WEDDING ETIQUETTE
PROPERLY EXPLAINED

WEDDING ETIQUETTE PROPERLY EXPLAINED

MARRIAGE UNDER ALL DENOMINATIONS

BY

VERNON HEATON

PAPERFRONTS

ELLIOT RIGHT WAY BOOKS
KINGSWOOD SURREY UK

SALE CONDITIONS

This book shall only be sold, lent or hired for profit, trade or otherwise in its original binding, except where special permission has been granted by the publishers.
While the author and publisher strive to ensure accuracy in this book, they regret they cannot be held responsible for any errors there may be.

Made and printed in Great Britain by C. Nicholls & Company Ltd.,
Manchester 11

CONTENTS

INTRODUCTION

THE overwhelming majority of the population take the marriage vows at least once during their lifetime.

In anticipation of that romantic event most girls, during their impressionable 'teens, take a few starry-eyed peeps between the pages of their prayer books to browse through the Marriage Service.

The men, of course, pretend a lesser romance and express to all who will heed them, almost to the point of no return, their intention of evading the "walk up the aisle".

But the result is usually the same; some registrar, somewhere, sometime will link their names in his register with those of their partners. And when that time comes, the man will willingly – or unwillingly – fall into line with his future wife's insistent wishes that the wedding be solemnized with all the ancient tradition and ceremony that she will claim as her right.

Yet, despite the seriousness of the step and the "so long as ye both shall live" finality of their vows, few engaged couples give much thought to the legal obligations involved.

7

This book is therefore designed to satisfy the bride's eager wish to know and so be able to follow the exact details of the formalities and the long established customs expected of a wedding – and to at least give the bridegroom some little insight into the legal requirements that must be met before a marriage can take place.

With the passing of the years, though the laws concerning marriage and the subsequent responsibilities of a man and his wife towards one another, have changed considerably, the etiquette has varied but little. Only in the selection of a marriage partner has the modern girl succeeded in breaking through the strict social conventions of her grandmother's day. The rest of the rites survive in the ritual of the service and the pageantry of the "day", – with only the possible exception of the bride's election to be excused the vow "to obey".

In those bygone days a girl would have little say in the so very important matter of choosing her own husband. If she came from a "good" family she would have been so closely chaperoned that there would have been very few opportunities for her to mix with the younger members of the male sex, and however amenable her parents might have been – or rather, her father might have been – she would have had very little experience on which to make her choice.

And the young man who, though he had had the opportunity of meeting quite a bevy of eligible young ladies, would rarely have been afforded the privilege of a private conversation with any one of them. The result was that when the time came for him to approach a girl's father with a request to be allowed to offer her his "hand and his heart", his choice of the maiden was likely to have been based on nothing more emotional than her pretty face, her social status and the depth of her father's purse.

And in due course as he knelt before her, she would most probably have received his: "I have the honour to lay at your feet . . . ", in fluttering excitement and reply breathlessly: "I thank you for the honour you have done me and . . . ", knowing that the young man had been approved by her father – otherwise he would never have been given the opportunity to make his proposal.

And perhaps because she would be kept in ignorance of any alternative suitor, perhaps too because she was rising twenty, her acceptance of the kneeling swain could almost have been taken for granted – happily or otherwise.

Today, the proposal is likely to be made without any reference to either sets of parents and may very well consist of the young man's: "What about it?", and his beloved's unflurried: "Why not?" in acceptance.

But the sincerity of both will probably be the deeper because neither will be entering the compact entirely ignorant of the other's character, and neither will have been dragooned into the engagement.

From that moment on the prospective bridegroom will be on "pins-and-needles" until the whole business is over and done with. He will be glad to know, and very ready to point out to his bride-to-be, that the legal requirements for a marriage are simple so long as each is free to marry the other and that they are both over 21 or have their parents consent. All that is necessary is for the banns or intention to marry to be published and then, in due time, for them to spend less than ten minutes in front of a Registrar and two witnesses, and to sign the register thereafter.

But almost always he will find it useless to point out to his bride that all the ancient trappings, religious services and public receptions in the world, will do nothing towards making the marriage more binding either in law or in social acceptance. She will most surely expect to be allowed to pass from her parents care to that of her husband with all due ceremony; she will wish to meet all her friends on that day of days, to receive their good wishes – a bride is never "congratulated" – and she will not easily be persuaded to surrender her undoubted right to queen it for a day.

But to whom can she turn for details of the ceremonial, of the prescribed protocol and of the established order of events of the great occasion? Her parents would seem to be the obvious source of information, of course, but their memories of their own wedding will be twenty or more years dim.

Their friends? Are they absolutely sure?

Why not within these pages?

CHAPTER ONE

CAN YOU MARRY A RELATION? THE LEGAL POINTS

CERTAIN marriages are prohibited where the couple are held to be too closely related. The Book of Common Prayer lists the forbidden marriages as follows:–

A man may not marry his

mother, daughter, father's mother, mother's mother, son's daughter, daughter's daughter, sister, father's daughter, mother's daughter, wife's mother, wife's daughter, father's wife, son's wife, father's father's wife, mother's father's wife, wife's father's mother, wife's mother's mother, wife's son's daughter, wife's daughter's daughter, son's son's wife, daughter's son's wife, father's sister, mother's sister, brother's daughter or sister's daughter.

A woman may not marry her

Father, son, father's father, mother's father, son's son, brother, father's son, mother's son, husband's father, husband's son, mother's husband, daughter's husband, father's mother's husband, mother's mother's husband, husband's father's father, husband's mother's father, husband's son's son, husband's daughter's son,

son's daughter's husband, daughter's daughter's husband, father's brother, mother's brother, brother's son or sister's son.

Marriage Acts were promulgated in Parliament in 1907 and 1921 permitting a man's marriage to his deceased wife's sister, deceased brother's widow, deceased wife's brother's daughter, deceased wife's sister's daughter, father's deceased brother's widow, mother's deceased brother's widow, deceased wife's father's sister, deceased wife's mother's sister, brother's deceased son's widow and sister's deceased son's widow.

A clergyman has the right to refuse to solemnize any marriage where the degree of relationship between the couple is forbidden by the church, but if he so wishes he may allow another minister to use his church for the purpose.

A Registrar of Marriages, however, must marry a couple so long as they are legally entitled to marry.

If either party has been married previously, he or she must produce to the Registrar of Marriages documentary proof of their legal ability to re-marry. Where the original partner has died a death certificate is necessary to establish that proof, and where he or she has been divorced, the decree absolute is required. A decree *nisi* is not enough in England and Wales. In Scotland a divorce becomes absolute as soon as it is granted.

In England and Wales both parties to a marriage

must have reached the age of 21 (although legislation is going through to reduce this age to 18), unless they have the consent of their parents, or guardians. Such permission must be given in writing and signed by both the minor's parents or guardians.

Where the parents or guardians are abroad their signatures to the letter of consent need to be properly witnessed, usually by a notary public or perhaps a consul.

Where there is neither a parent nor a guardian, a minor has the right to apply to the courts for permission to marry and similarly, where he or she feels that a parent's or guardian's permission is being unreasonably refused, an application to overrule their decision can be made to the same court.

In Scotland the age of consent is 16 and for that reason Scotland, particularly the traditional Gretna Green, continues to be the mecca for those resident in other parts of Europe, who are under 21 and have been refused their parents' consent.

To qualify for marriage under Scottish law those wishing to be married there must have resided in that country for not less than twenty-one days immediately prior to the wedding.

In all cases there must be at least two witnesses to the marriage – excluding the Minister and the Registrar.

CHAPTER TWO

MODERN ENGAGEMENT DETAILS

An engagement is a much less formal affair than it was in the years gone by. It is still a contract, of course, though not in itself unbreakable without recourse to law.

However, losses caused to either party, through the other calling off the engagement, may well become the subject of a legal wrangle. This usually takes the form of a claim by the disappointed girl against the man who has broken off their engagement, for the cost of perhaps, the linen, the bedding and other household items she has bought from her own savings towards their joint home. She may add to that any debts she has incurred towards the wedding arrangements, such as the reception, that cannot readily be cancelled – and for any other expenses she has contracted in consequence of the promise of marriage.

If, on the other hand, it is the girl who has put an end to the engagement, the man may feel justified in claiming the return of the engagement ring he has bought her, and for the return of any other valuable pieces of jewellery that he may have presented to her on the understanding that she was to become his wife.

The claims of either party would only have substance however, if it could be proved that they were incurred only because of the wedding and represented nothing more than a financial loss because of the declared intention of one or other of them not to proceed with the marriage.

Damages for breach of promise are unlikely to succeed today and consequently the prospect of being able to heal a broken heart with a nice fat cheque is too remote to be worth more than a moment's thought – and surely, a broken engagement is far, far better than to become the unwanted partner in an unhappy marriage?

Usually, an engagement is accepted nowadays merely as a public expression of the intention of a man and a girl to marry. The announcement being necessary to justify their joint absence from many of the gatherings of their friends, to establish their wish to be invited to parties as a couple – and to make it clear that neither of them remains free to listen to further proposals of marriage.

Parents are not heeded so carefully, or always informed, before the modern girl and her man decide to announce their engagement. Much of this attitude is due to the high earning capacity of today's young man – and indeed, that of his fiancée – and they are therefore less dependent on their parents.

However, parents are still entitled to some courtesy and as the odds are that they will in any event pay for the wedding and the reception – if nothing more – it is perhaps wise not to jeopardize their goodwill through negligence and bad manners.

Correctly, the bride's parents should be the first to be told of the decision. To ask their "consent" is no longer general – unless, of course, the girl is under age. Then follows the man's parents – and thereafter the announcement may be broadcast as widely as the couple should desire.

The formality of an announcement in the press is much less rare than it used to be; most people are told as and when the couple happen to meet them. But if the announcement is made through the newspapers, it is proper to inform relatives and close friends verbally in advance.

The next consideration is the engagement ring. It is thought to set the seal on the betrothal of the pair and is in itself a warning to other young men not to poach.

However, though an engagement ring is still the prized possession of most girls who have "found their man" – and remains the prized token of those who have subsequently married – its intrinsic value is perhaps less of an assurance of the young man's depth of feeling today, than of the common sense of the pair who have taken into careful consideration their financial station, prospects and intentions.

Many engaged couples give a lot of thought to the amount that should be spent from their resources on such practical things as a down payment on a house, the quantity and quality of furniture they can afford to purchase before entering too deeply into hire purchase commitments and even whether or not they should own a car – before estimating what will be left with which to buy the symbol of their engagement.

But however intrinsically valueless the ring, its symbolic superstitition makes it almost a "must".

But instead of the more usual diamonds, it is common for a couple to set aside only a limited sum for the ring and economize by selecting a cheaper stone. A paste imitation is always considered to be both in poor taste and unlucky, but where it is suitable and cheap enough, a girl may choose her own birthstone with propriety.

Birthstones are generally accepted as being for the

January girl,	Garnets, meaning	Constancy
February	Amethysts	Sincerity
March	Bloodstones	Courage
April	Diamonds	Purity
May	Emeralds	Hope
June	Pearls or Agates	Health
July	Rubies	Passion
August	Sardonyx	Married Happiness
September	Sapphires	Repentance
October	Opals	A Lovable Nature
November	Topaz	Cheerfulness
December	Turquoise or Lapis Lazuli	Unselfishness

In return it is usual for the girl to give her betrothed an engagement present – again, of course, limited in value to the means at her disposal after more practical matters have been considered. A cigarette case, a lighter or some piece of jewellery such as a ring are the more usual gifts for such an occasion.

Though the engaged couple are expected from now on to be kept very busy with the arrangements for their future; the wedding itself, the reception afterwards, the honeymoon, their new home and the furniture that is needed for it – even the trivialities of negotiations with the Electricity Board, the Gas Board and so on and so on, they still have to give some thought to their social obligations.

The engagement party is the most urgent of these and it usually takes place on the day the announcement is made in the press or shortly afterwards. It is at that party that the official announcement of the engagement is made – if it has not already been published in the press.

It is obvious that the engagement party should be held at a very early date after the decision of the couple to marry. It would be difficult to maintain the secret for long in any event and the party loses a lot of its glamour if it is staged long after everybody knows the reason for it and all the congratulations and good wishes have been expressed.

Long engagements are often considered both un-necessary and a little undignified, but if the wedding is to be conducted with all the trappings, on a day and time convenient to most of the guests and to book a reception to follow, a certain lapse of time is necessary. Many couples are anxious to marry; all of them seem to prefer much the same date and reception rooms, the same honeymoon hotels and even the same photographer – which means that a good deal of planning is necessary before arrangements can be finalized.

The engagement party is usually a most informal affair and leaves the couple with a wide choice of methods at their disposal. Again the first consideration must be the cost, though it is quite usual for the bride's parents to pay for it, whatever the scale. But as the same people are generally expected to have to pay for the wedding reception in due course, it can be quite a strain on them if thought isn't given to the matter from the very beginning.

The party may be held at either of the parents' homes, though again it is more usual to hold it at the bride's home. It is her father who makes the official announcement of the engagement.

It might be confined to a family party of say, both sets of parents, brothers and sisters – and maybe those grandparents who are able to be there. The numbers can be increased, of course, though a lot of care must be exercised in the selection. Aunts are inclined to be upset if they have been left out for a close friend and close friends are likely to be resentful if some long neglected relative is included instead of them. Tact is essential.

Of course the numbers can be expanded *ad infinitum* by taking a hall for the occasion, but it is better to make the occasion as intimate as possible. If larger numbers are to be invited than it is possible to cater for at home, a restaurant is the better place for the party. Everything is supplied, cooked and served – and even the bride's mother has a chance to enjoy herself.

However, even here the guests should be selected with care. It is quite usual for the young couple and their equally young friends to go on from the dinner party in the restaurant – or even from their home – to perhaps a dance or a night club afterwards. And the older generation will not be expected to accompany them. Nor should the parents resent being abandoned by the younger element.

The arrangements for the party in a restaurant or an hotel are quite straightforward. The hotelier or the *restaurateur* will advise you of exactly what you should do to make the occasion a success. He will advise on the menu, the table decorations, the seating, the wines and even on the speeches if the host is at all doubtful about the procedure.

The meal itself need not be too costly, depending of course on the menu, the standard of the hotel or restaurant and the style of the service. Wines will add considerably to the bill if a lot of discretion is not used. Nor is it necessary to have wines. Perhaps a sherry or port with the speeches – and always of course, orange-ades or other soft drinks.

For those who might like to spread their wings on the party I have made a few suggestions for menus in a subsequent chapter and have indicated what wines could be served with them both economically and as a "grand gesture".

The young couple will of course be given the place of honour at the table and if the party is given at home, they will be excused from the usual chores of service and washing-up afterwards. The bride's parents will sit next to her while the bridegroom's will find their places at his side. This of course will be varied at the wedding reception after they are married. The bride will sit on her groom's left side as always.

The only speeches that are required are two. The first will be made by the bride's father when he either announces the engagement of his daughter or wishes them both Health and Happiness. The bridegroom replies on behalf of himself and his bride in proposing the health of their parents.

The speeches are usually light-hearted as it is a happy occasion and other toasts may be drunk if the mood of the party permits.

If the younger people are to go on elsewhere or are to dance at the hotel where the engagement party has been given, a move should be made immediately after the speeches. Either by the couple who will lead their friends away or by the parents who will leave their children to their own devices – depending on whether the further entertainment is to be held there or else-where.

As the party is informal dress it is usually lounge suits for the men and semi-evening wear for the women. Printed invitations are unusual, unless the party is to be wide in scope, and even hand-written invitations are the exception, the telephone being the usual thing.

Place-cards and a table plan are considered unnecessary too. Everybody knows that the engaged couple will occupy the seats of honour and that their parents will sit on either side of them. After that, the bride's father, as the host, will suggest where his guests should sit as they come to the table.

Of course a wise host will know his guests in advance – or find out about those he does not know. This enables him to know who should sit next to whom; it could be pretty disastrous to sit old enemies next to one another! But he still must pay regard to the custom that the sexes should alternate.

Sometimes it happens that the girl and her betrothed come from far apart; maybe the man is a Londoner and his wife to be, an Edinburgh girl. Obviously it is impossible to bring everybody who has a to be at the party all the way from London, but as the bride's parents are the hosts, the venue will almost certainly be in Scotland. In such an event the girl should try and make it possible to attend a similar party in London. This party will be entirely informal, usually at the home of the man's parents and limited to those who were unable to travel north for the official party.

If this is not practicable, the duty still remains on the couple to bring the two sets of parents together round a table – wherever it can be arranged. And at that gathering there will be no need to invite anyone else – with the possible exception of brothers and sisters and grandparents.

CHAPTER THREE

ACCEPTING that the couple fulfil the legal qualifications set out in Chapter 1, they must then decide on the form their marriage is to take.

Broadly, they have the choice of being married:

1. in accordance with the rites of the Church of England.

2. in accordance with the rites of any other religious denomination

3. before a Superintendent Registrar of Marriages in accordance with the Civil Law and without any religious service.

Church of England. Those who wish to be married according to the rites of the Church of England will be expected to have been baptized, though not of necessity by a minister of the Church of England. Nor are they wholly debarred from having their wedding solemnized in church because they were not baptized in their youth; there is no reason why they should not receive baptism at any time before the marriage.

The venue of the marriage must be in the parish where the couple reside, or if they belong to different parishes, in the parish church of either one of them.

Custom decrees that weddings are solemnized in the parish church of the bride, though this is a matter of tradition and not of law. It is a convenient custom too, as apart from the symbolism of the man coming to collect his bride, it gives her a chance to say farewell to her friends if she is going elsewhere to live, and it makes the question of the arrangements for the reception afterwards a simple matter for the bride's parents.

It might happen however that one or the other of the couple have been in the habit of worshipping in a church outside the parish in which he or she lives. In such case the wedding may be conducted in that church so long as the party concerned worships regularly there for not less than six months. This would entitle the party concerned to sign the electoral roll of that parish, giving them the right of membership – including the right to be married there.

There are four ways in which a marriage can be authorized to take place in a church of the Church of England:

(*a*) by Banns

(*b*) by Common Licence

(*c*) by Special Licence

(*d*) by a certificate issued by a Superintendent Registrar of Marriages.

(*a*) The most usual proceedure is by the reading of the banns on three successive Sundays in the parish church of each of the engaged couple – or, of course, in the parish where one or the other of them has signed the electoral roll.

Naturally, an application must be made to the incumbent of the church in which the couple desire to be married. Only one of them need make the application. If the minister is satisfied that the couple are legally qualified to marry, he will arrange to give notice of their intention to the members of his congregation after the second lesson on each of the Sundays concerned, permitting anyone who may have reason to doubt their qualifications to make an objection.

The banns must, of course, be read in the parish church of both the man and the girl, if they reside in different parishes – and they must continue to reside in their particular parishes for the whole of the three weeks during which the banns are read.

The minister due to perform the ceremony will require a certificate from the clergyman of the church not being the actual venue of the wedding, but being the parish church of the other of the couple, certifying that the banns have in fact been published there too, and that no valid objection has been received.

After the banns have been read for the three specified Sundays without any substantiated objection being voiced, the marriage can be solemnized at any time between 8 a.m. and 6 p.m. on almost any day thereafter. However, there is a time limit of three calendar months to the effectiveness of this authority – and the banns must again be called if the wedding is still intended to take place.

The cost of a marriage in a Church of England place of worship under the procedure will be:

Cost of banns, including publishing them, 17/6.

The marriage certificate, 17/6.

The marriage fee can be from 25/- upwards; depending whether choir, bells etc. are required, the total can approach or even exceed £20.

(b) Marriage by Common Licence is usually where the three weeks delay taken up in the reading of the banns is, for some reason or another, not tolerable. The reason for haste may be legion; a hurried move abroad by the bridgroom to take up a particular post, perhaps; or maybe because of a family illness or, too often, because a birth is imminent. Whatever the reason, there is no need for delay nor to declare the reason for the short notice.

Nor are residential qualifications so strict. Only one of the couple need live in the parish where the marriage is to be conducted, and he or she need only have resided in the district for fifteen days, immediately prior to the application. The other party to the marriage is not called upon to produce any residential qualifications.

Only a clear day's notice need be given before the ceremony, thereafter the actual date and time is a matter of arrangement between the couple and the minister – with a time limit of three calendar months to the effectiveness of the authority. A new application would have to be made if the marriage had not taken place within that time and it was still intended to go ahead with the ceremony.

The application for such a licence may be made to the incumbent of the church where it is desired to hold the wedding. If he is not able to grant the licence himself, he will be able to advise the couple of the address of the nearest Surrogate for granting Marriage Licences in the Diocese, or it may be made to the Faculty Office, 1 The Sanctuary, Westminster, London S.W.1.

The application must be made in person, though only one of the parties to the wedding need do so.

The Licence usually costs about £2-15-0.

(c) Marriage by Special Licence is most unusual and such a licence is only issued on the authority of the Archbishop of Canterbury through the Faculty Office, 1 The Sanctuary, Westminster, London S.W.1.

Such a licence would only be granted in the case of emergency and where an ordinary licence would not suffice. The usual reason for the issue of such a licence is because neither of the couple have residential qualifications, or more often, because there is some urgent reason why the ceremony needs to be held outside a church licensed for marriages, or a Register

Office or other authorized place; perhaps by a bedside in a hospital or a home where there is a serious illness – to the point of death.

Strangely, neither St. Paul's Cathedral, Westminster Abbey nor the chapel of Buckingham Palace is registered for marriages and weddings conducted therein, even of Royalty, require the Archbishop of Canterbury's Special Licence.

The Licence costs not less than about £25.

(*d*) It is possible to obtain a certificate of authorization for a marriage to be conducted in a church of the Church of England, but this would not be binding on the incumbent who might well insist on a Surrogate's Licence being procured.

In any event it would seem wise to consult the minister of the church first – and he may find it difficult because of prior commitments to find a suitable time for the ceremony.

However, if the clergyman is willing to accept such a certificate, no further legal authorization would be needed.

Such an application needs to be made to the Superintendent Registrar not less than 21 days before the wedding is expected to take place and each of the parties to it must have been resident for not less than seven days in their own district immediately before the notice is entered by the Registrar.

Once the certificate has been issued it is valid for

three calendar months; if the wedding is to take place after that time, a new application to the Registrar must be made.

The cost of a Superintendent Registrar's certificate is £1-13-0, if both the bride and the bridegroom reside in the same district; if they live in different districts the charge will be £1-16-0.

The Marriage Certificate will cost 3/9. The marriage fee is usually about 25/-, though it may vary considerably.

The Roman Catholic Church. Where both the man and the girl are Roman Catholics a certificate must be obtained from the Superintendent Registrar of Marriages of the district in which they live, which will also be the district in which they marry. Only one of the parties need attend personally on the Registrar to make the application, but he or she must give all the essential details concerning both; ages, residential qualifications, addresses – and where necessary proof of either divorce or the death of a previous partner.

Divorce is frowned on by the Roman Catholic Church and only in the rarest of circumstances will a re-marriage be countenanced. It is possible however that the divorced party was originally married in a Register Office and perhaps for that reason, the marriage is not recognized and there will therefore be no bar to the projected wedding, so long as the Civil Law has been met.

If the engaged couple live in different districts, notice must be given to the Registrar of Marriages in both, and to establish their residential qualifications, they must each have resided in the district where his or her application is to be made for at least seven days prior to the notice being entered by the Registrar.

Twenty-one days thereafter the Registrar will issue the required certificates – providing that neither notices have resulted in valid objections being raised.

Where it is desired to hold the wedding ceremony within the prescribed twenty-one days after the entry of the notice, the Superintendent Registrar may issue a Common Licence together with his certificate. This entitles the couple to marry at any time after the elapse of one clear day after the notice has been given.

Where a Common Licence is sought, only one of the engaged couple need have residential qualifications, but it consists of the need for that person to have lived for not less than fifteen days continuously in the district where the application is made, immediately prior to the notice being given to the Registrar.

It is well to consult the parish priest concerning the detailed arrangements for the wedding as, though the Registrar's certificate authorizes the marriage under the Civil Law, it does not insist that the church shall carry out the ceremony.

The Roman Catholic Church still requires that the banns be read in the parish church of each of the betrothed – except in the event of one of them not being a Catholic. In such case, no banns are read.

There are differing types of service to solemnize matrimony too, dependent upon the time of the year and where one or other of the parties is a non-Catholic.

Generally speaking, a Catholic priest will require two or three months' notice of the projected wedding and where one of them is a non-Catholic perhaps longer. He will require time to give the non-Catholic several periods of instruction before he will give the necessary Dispensation permitting the marriage of a Catholic to a non-Catholic.

Adequate notice is also required by the ministers of the various *non-established churches*, such as the Methodists, Baptists, Presbyterians and Congregationalists, of marriages intended to be celebrated in their churches.

To comply with the Civil Law all marriages must take place within a church or a building registered by the Superintendent Registrar of Marriages for the purpose of conducting marriage services. Such marriages must be witnessed by at least two people who have reached the age of 21 and by an "authorized person".

The "authorized person" will be the Registrar, his deputy or more usually a minister of the church who has been authorized by the Registrar.

Many of the Free Churches are registered under the Marriage Acts but some are not; most of the ministers of these churches are "authorized", but by no means all of them.

It is obviously necessary to check on these points, so that the couple when applying to the Registrar for a certificate, can arrange for the civil ceremony to take place in the Register Office in advance of the church wedding, where the church is not registered for the conduct of marriages, or to inform the Superintendent Registrar of the need for his, or his deputy's presence at the church, where it is registered, but where the minister performing the ceremony is not an "authorized person".

The fact that a minister is not an authorized person does not preclude him from conducting the marriage service, but it does require the attendance of the Superintendent Registrar or his deputy.

The details of the conditions attached to the issue of a Superintendent Registrar's certificate and licence have been described elsewhere in this chapter and need not be repeated.

The Civil Law is varied in the case of a *Jewish Wedding* to permit the ceremony to take place anywhere; in a synagogue, a private house, a hired hall or indeed in any chosen place whether or not it is registered for the purpose. Nor are there any specified times during which the service may be held – though it is usual nowadays for the ceremony to be performed in a synagogue at any convenient time, excluding the hours between sunset on a Friday and sunset on the following Saturday; the Jewish Sabbath.

The application to the Superintendent Registrar for the certificate and licence is made in the same way as for all other denominations, and in all respects other than those quoted in the last paragraph, the conditions for their issue are the same.

A *Quaker Wedding* requires, of course, the same recourse to a Superintendent Registrar for a certificate as in all cases, other than that applicable to a marriage by banns in accordance with the rites of the Church of England.

It requires too, the completion of certain Marriage Forms obtained from the Registering Officer of the liberating Monthly Meeting. That is the Monthly Meetin place where the girl is a member, or alternatively, the Meeting place where she lives.

Form A is the signed declaration of the parties to marry and details the time and place of the wedding.

Only one of the parties need be a member of the Society of Friends, but the other is acceptable so long as he or she is in sympathy with the testimony and nature of the character of the marriage and can produce two recommendations in writing from full members.

Notice of the intended marriage is given at the close of the Sunday morning meetings where each of the parties are members or where they usually worship or even in the district where they live.

If no written notice of objection has been received

after seven days, the Registering Officer completes a form to this effect, and arrangements for the wedding can then proceed.

Civil Ceremony. There is no need for a marriage to be solemnized either in a place of worship or by a minister of religion. Only the Civil Law need be heeded and such a marriage in a Register Office, conducted by a Registrar of Marriages, is as completely binding in law as any conducted under the auspices of any religious body – and is as difficult to dissolve.

There are many reasons why a couple may elect to be married in a Register Office under Civil Law alone; they may subscribe to no religious beliefs, they may be of different persuasions and prefer to marry under a neutral authority, they may be debarred by the Church because one or both have been divorced – and there are those who, for one reason or another, wish to keep the marriage as close a secret as possible.

Absolute secrecy is not, of course, possible as the intention to marry is published by an entry in the Registrar's "notice book" which is available for all to inspect. However such an inspection is rarely made by unsuspecting parties, and it is unusual, except where the couple are personalities who attract the attention of the press, for the intention to leak out in advance.

For such a marriage, application must be made to the Superintendent Registrar of Marriages in the district where the couple live and where they intend to marry.

Such an application must be made in person and a detailed application form must be completed.

The form calls for information concerning the names, ages, addresses with the period each has resided there, and a declaration must be added stating that there is no legal objection to the marriage.

If either of the parties is under 21 years of age, the consent in writing of both parents is required.

Both parties to the marriage must have lived in the district where they make their application to marry, for at least seven days immediately preceding the entry in the Superintendent Registrar's notice book. If they come from different districts, separate applications must be made in each and the residential qualification will apply to each, in his or her own district.

If either of the parties has been married previously, he or she will will have to produce proof to the Superintendent Registrar, either in the form of a death certificate or a decree absolute, that there is no legal barrier to a second marriage.

If no objection is received and verified within twenty-one days of the notice, the Registrar will issue his certificate and the marriage can be conducted as soon thereafter as is convenient.

If, for some reason or other, the couple wish to be married within the prescribed twenty-one days, they may apply to the Superintendent Registrar for a Common Licence. The conditions for its issue are similar to those required for the certificate, except that only one of the parties need make the application and that that party has been resident in the district for not less than fifteen days immediately preceding the entry of the intention in the notice book.

If there is no objection, the licence and the certificate will be issued one clear day after the application and the marriage can take place in the Register Office at any time thereafter.

Serving members of the *Royal Navy* who are seagoing are not penalized by their inability to establish residential qualifications ashore. In any such case the sailor may make application to his Captain to have the banns read aboard his ship during morning service on three successive Sundays; the banns also being read in the bride's church, where the ceremony will eventually take place, at the same time.

At the end of the qualifying period of twenty-one days, the Captain will make an entry in his Banns of Marriage register and issue a certificate stating that the banns have been called and that no valid objections to the marriage have been brought to his attention. This certificate must then be passed to the minister ashore who is to perform the wedding ceremony.

When it is intended that the marriage should take place before a Registrar of Marriages in a Register Office, or before a minister of a church other than that of the Church of England, the seaman should complete a form of notice in the presence of his Captain and that Officer should countersign it as a witness.

At the same time, the bride must give similar notice to the Superintendent Registrar in the district where she lives and where the marriage is to be conducted, and to the officiating minister if a church service is intended.

After twenty-one days the Captain will issue a certificate informing the Superintendent Registrar that due notice was given him by the seaman, and that no valid objection had been brought to his notice.

As in all other cases, the authority obtained is limited to three calendar months, and if the marriage is to take place after the expiry of that period, fresh notice must be given.

CHAPTER FOUR

LIVING ABROAD, FOREIGNERS, IRISH, SCOTTISH, ETC.

MARRIAGE Regulations and Laws differ in other parts of the United Kingdom. Nor are they the same for foreigners marrying in the United Kingdom, nor do they apply in quite the same way to British subjects marrying abroad. Complications arise where a British subject intends to marry a foreigner – abroad or at home – and there is always the matter of the girl's nationality after her marriage.

This chapter is designed to disentangle some of the strands from the web of requirements, but the engaged couple would be well advised to consult the various authorities. In Britain an interview should be sought with the clergyman or leader of the religious sect involved. If there is to be no religious service, advice will be available at the various Registrars of Marriages offices, the addresses of which may be found in the local telephone directory.

If a British subject intends to marry abroad, he or she should consult a member of the British Embassy, Legation or Consulate in the country and district where the marriage is to take place; irrespective of whether both parties are British, or one of them happens to be a national of the country concerned.

Similarly, a foreigner wishing to marry in the United Kingdom, whether to a British subject or to someone of their own nationality, should consult his or her resident representative in Britain to make sure that their marriage will be accepted as legally binding in their own country.

NORTHERN IRELAND

Church of Ireland. A marriage may be authorized to take place in a church of the Church of Ireland in four different manners:

    (*a*) by Banns
    (*b*) by Licence
    (*c*) by Special Licence
    (*d*) by a certificate issued by a Registrar of
        Marriages.

(*a*) Where both parties to the marriage are Protestant Episcopalians, the banns may be read in the church where the ceremony is to take place, subject to the rites of the church. The clergyman who is expected to conduct the service must be consulted about the arrangements.

(*b*) A Licence may be obtained from a Licenser of the Church of Ireland under the following conditions:

1. One or both of the parties must be Protestant Episcopalians.

2. One at least of the couple must have resided for not less than seven days in the district where the notice is

given to the Licenser, immediately preceding the service of the notice.

3. The Licenser will send copies of the notice to the ministers of each of the churches where the parties usually worship – and seven days after the service of the notice on him, he will issue his certificate.

4. One or other of the parties must take an oath, or declaration, that his or her usual place of residence is within the district attached to the church where the marriage is to be solemnized – and that he or she has lived there for not less than 14 days immediately preceding the declaration.

The address of the District Church of Ireland Licenser can be obtained from the clergyman at the church where the ceremony is to take place.

(c) A Special Licence may be granted by a Bishop of the Church of Ireland, provided one or both of the partners to the marriage are Protestant Episcopalians. This authorizes the marriage to take place at any time and in any place within the jurisdiction of the Bishop.

(d) A Registrar's Certificate may be obtained, where one or both of the parties are Protestant Episcopalians, authorizing the marriage to take place in a church. The application for the certificate must be made to the Registrar in the district where the couple live. If they live in different districts, the Registrar in each of them must provide a certificate.

The Registrar must send a notice to the church's

incumbent where each of the couple worships and if different to either of these, to the minister of the church where the service is to be held.

At least one of the parties must have resided in the district attached to the church where the marriage is to be celebrated, for not less than 14 days immediately preceding the declaration of the fact.

Presbyterian Churches. Though the rites and ceremonies of the various constituent churches differ somewhat, the authorities for the celebration of marriages are similar. They are obtained by:

(*a*) Banns.

(*b*) Licence.

(*c*) Special Licence.

(*a*) Banns may be published in the church or the churches where the couple normally worship. The ministers concerned will each require 6 days' notice of the intention, after which they will read the banns to their congregations on the following three successive Sundays.

The wedding must take place in one of the churches where the banns have been published.

(*b*) To obtain a Licence, one or both of the parties to the marriage must be Presbyterians.

Application must first be made to the minister of the congregation of which one of them has been a member for the past month. He will then issue a certificate to that effect, which should be produced to the Licensing Minister appointed by the Presbytery, seven days before he is expected to grant the licence.

Before the grant of the licence, he or she, whoever has obtained the certificate from the minister, must state on Oath, or make a Declaration to the effect that one or other of the parties has resided for fifteen days, immediately preceding, within the Presbytery.

(c) A Special Licence may be obtained authorizing the marriage to take place at any time or place in Ireland. The issuing authority is the Moderator of the Presbyterian Church of Ireland, or the Moderators of several other Presbyterian bodies.

One or both of the parties to the marriage must be a member of the congregational body headed by the Moderator granting the licence.

The Roman Catholic Church. The Irish Marriage Acts authorize the following procedures for marriages by Roman Catholics:

(a) by Licence

(b) by a certificate from a Registrar.

(a) Where both parties are Roman Catholics a licence may be obtained from a Licenser appointed by a Bishop of the church of Rome. Application must be made to the Licenser not less than seven days before the ceremony and copies of the Notice must be sent by him to the priests in charge of the churches where each of them have been in the habit of worshipping.

(*b*) When one of the parties is other than a Roman Catholic, a Registrar's Certificate may be obtained authorizing the marriage to take place in a Roman Catholic church.

Other Religious Bodies. Three forms of authorization for a marriage are available to the members of other churches:

    (*a*) by Registrar's Certificate
    (*b*) by Licence
    (*c*) by Special Licence.

(*a*) A Registrar's Certificate is obtainable after twenty-one clear days notice of the intention to marry. The notice must be given to the Registrar in the district where both have lived for not less than seven days immediately prior to the application, each of them must have lived in their particular district for not less than seven days immediately preceding the notice.

In the former case the Registrar must send copies of the Notice to the minister of the church where they both worship and to the minister of the church where they are to be married – if that be different. Where they live in differing districts the Registrar must send copies of the Notice to the clergymen of each place of worship attended by one or other of the parties and of course to the minister appointed to conduct the marriage service.

(*b*) If the wedding is to be held at shorter notice than that applicable under a Registrar's Certificate, a licence may be obtained from the District Registrar. This permits the solemnization of the marriage seven clear days after the issue of the licence.

To be eligible for such a licence the parties, if they live in different districts, must have been resident there for not less than fifteen days immediately preceding the giving of notice to the Registrar; if they live in the same district, one must have resided there for fifteen days and the other at least seven days prior to the giving of the Notice.

The Registrar must send a copy of the Notice to the Registrar of the district where the other of the pair happens to reside, or to the minister of the churches concerned – and, of course, to the minister due to perform the ceremony.

(c) A Special Licence may be granted by the heads of most of the Protestant Churches, authorizing the marriages of those who are either in an unusual hurry or who wish to marry in a less usual place than a church; perhaps a hospital or a home.

A Special Licence permits the wedding to take place at any time and in any place – in Ireland.

Jews. Marriages between Jews require the authorization of a Registrar's Certificate, but they need not marry in the district where they live.

Special Licences are not issued to Jews.

Quakers. Members of the Society of Friends may apply

to a Registrar for either a Licence or a Special Licence, which are issued on similar conditions to those of Other Denominations.

Civil Marriages. Where a couple desire to be married without any religious ceremony, they may apply to a Registrar to be married within a Registry Office.

The conditions are similar to those applicable for the issue of either a Licence or a Special Licence, except that instead of informing the ministers concerned, the Registrar must send a copy of the notice to the Registrar of the district in which either of them may live, which is not his own.

Where one of the parties is resident outside Northern Ireland. Where both parties are Protestant Episcopalians who wish to be married in accordance with the rites of the Church of Ireland, banns must be read on three successive Sundays in the parish church of the district in Ireland in which one of them lives and where the marriage is to be solemnized. If the second party to the wedding is resident in either England or Wales, banns should be read similarly in the parish church of the district in which he or she lives.

If the couple intend to marry in a church where a Registrar's Certificate is necessary; that is, in a church of any other denomination or in a Registry Office; the party in Ireland must give seven days notice to the Registrar of the district in which he or she lives, and the one living in England or Wales must do similarly in his or her country.

A certificate from the Registrar in England or Wales must then be passed to the Registrar in Ireland; seven days later he will issue his certificate authorizing the marriage.

Where one of the parties to the marriage resides in Scotland, a certificate signed by the minister of the Scottish church stating that the banns have been read, is required by the Registrar in Northern Ireland; seven days after its receipt, the Registrar will authorize the marriage.

Where the marriage is to take place in England or Wales. Where a marriage is to be solemnized in either England or Wales and one of the parties is normally domiciled in Northern Ireland, a Registrar of the district in Ireland where that person lives must provide a certificate for the benefit of the Registrar or Clergyman in England or Wales, where the marriage is to take place.

If the marriage is to take place in Scotland no particular steps need be taken by the party resident in Northern Ireland. The couple need only comply with Scottish law.

SCOTLAND

There are two important differences between the Marriage Laws of England and Wales, and Scotland:

(*a*) Where the banns must be read in a Church of

England on three successive Sundays, only one Sunday is required by the Church of Scotland. However both parties should have resided in Scotland for not less than fifteen days prior to the wedding ceremony.

The residential qualifications may be varied so that only one of the parties possesses them where a church wedding is intended. The minister concerned may decide that although only one of the parties resides in Scotland, the other is sufficiently well-known to him either through personal knowledge or by repute, that he is willing to forego a certificate from the Registrar or minister of the district in which he resides.

This is not applicable where both parties to the wedding normally live in Scotland – nor is it compulsory for a minister to accept such a situation.

If neither party is normally resident in Scotland, both should proceed there and live in the country for at least fifteen days before giving notice to the Registrar. Alternatively, where only one goes to Scotland to establish residential qualifications and the other remains in England or Wales, the Superintendent Registrar in either of those countries will refuse to accept a notice until the other party has lived in Scotland for at least seven days. A further twenty-one days must elapse before he will issue his certificate for the benefit of the Registrar in Scotland.

If both parties live elsewhere than in the United Kingdom they must both establish residential qualifications in Scotland. There is no alternative available to them but to live in the country for the necessary fifteen days.

(*b*) In Scotland a youth or a girl, or both parties to a wedding, are eligible so long as they have reached their sixteenth birthday. No parental consent is required.

However, both must have the necessary residential qualifications in Scotland. If either party is resident in England or Scotland, the Registrar's Certificate in their home district will not be issued, unless that person is either over age, or produces written consent from his or her parents.

The establishment of residential qualifications in Scotland does not permit an immediate marriage; it merely entitles the applicants to give notice to the Registrar of their intention to marry. The Registrar then posts his notice on a public notice board and if there are no valid objections, he will issue his certificate after the lapse of eight clear days.

Marriage in the Church of Scotland. A marriage may be celebrated in the Church of Scotland after the banns have been read in the churches of each of the parties, in the districts where they possess the necessary legal residential qualifications, on a single Sunday. The minister's Certificate of Proclamation is issued forty-eight hours later.

The Minister may require that the banns be read on two successive Sundays, in which case the certificate will be issued on the day following the second reading.

Marriage of Other Denominations. Marriages within the rites of any other religious body are permitted either by the:

(*a*) Publication of a Notice
(*b*) Issue of a Sheriff's Licence.

Generally, the difference between the two procedures is concerned with the time that must elapse between the application to marry and the service itself.

(*a*) Publication by Notice is made at a Registrar's Office where a special form must be completed and signed by the party, or if they both live in the same district, by both parties, in the presence of two householders who must themselves sign as witnesses.

If the Registrar is satisfied that the notice in in order, he will post a copy of the notice on his notice board that same day. It must remain on view for eight clear days after which the Registrar will issue a Certificate of Publication, if no valid objections have been received by him.

The Certificate is valid for three months during which time the marriage can take place to suit the convenience of the couple and the minister conducting the service.

(*b*) A Sheriff's Licence is only granted in urgent or emergency conditions and is irrespective of whether the marriage is to be solemnized by a religious service or conducted as a civil ceremony. Both parties to the application must appear in person, probably with their legal adviser, before the Sheriff of the district where the marriage is to take place.

Before granting the Licence the Sheriff will satisfy himself:

1. That the circumstances are such that it is impossible for the couple to have the banns read in a church of the Church of Scotland, or by the Publication of a Notice in a Registrar's Office, because of the time factor. He will probably accept the excuse of a serious or dangerous illness as valid.

2. That at least one of the parties to the marriage has been resident in Scotland for not less than fifteen days immediately preceding the application.

3. And that there is no objection in law to the marriage.

A Sheriff's Licence is only valid for ten days after its issue.

Civil Marriages. A civil marriage is authorized either by Publication of Notice at a Registrar's Office, or by a Sheriff's Licence where haste is considered necessary.

Both procedures have been detailed in the preceding paragraphs.

Where one of the parties lives in England or Wales. The party living in either England or Wales should obtain a certificate of the publication of the banns from the minister concerned, or from a Superintendent Registrar of the district in which he or she lives. This certificate will be granted by the minister after the banns have been read on three successive Sundays, or by the Superintendent Registrar twenty-one days after he receives the notice of intention.

It is possible in the case of the party living in England or Wales who has a parent residing normally in Scotland, to have the banns read or the Notice published in the district of Scotland where that parent resides.

The party with Scottish residential qualification must make arrangments for the banns to be read in a church of the Church of Scotland, or by the Publication of a Notice at a Registrar's Office.

Where one of the parties lives in Northern Ireland or in Eire or in any foreign country. If such a person is to be married in Scotland, it is necessary for he or she to proceed to that country to establish residential qualifications, i.e., fifteen days, before an application can be made either to a minister of the Church of Scotland for the reading of banns, or to a Registrar for the Publication of a Notice.

However, if the party resident in Scotland makes application to the minister of his church, it is possible that that clergyman may accept the lack of a certificate or residential qualifications on the part of the other. If he does, usually because of personal knowledge of the party concerned, the Registrar will issue the necessary certificate. He must however satisfy himself that there appears to be no legal objection and must enter a

Marriage Schedule on the certificate of banns issued to the party resident in Scotland.

The minister cannot be compelled to accept such an application nor would it be granted where a civil marriage was contemplated.

Where neither parties resides in Scotland. If they both live in England or Wales, one of them must establish residential qualifications in Scotland by residing there for fifteen days immediately preceding the proclamation by banns, or the publication by notice in a Registrar's office.

In such event, the party continuing to reside in England or Wales, must obtain a certificate from the Superintendent Registrar of Marriages of that district. This certificate will not be issued until the party in Scotland has been resident there for seven days, and a further twenty-one days must elapse after that fact has been established.

The minister publishing the banns, or the Superintendent Registrar in England or Wales, will need to be satisfied that the party making the application to him is over age, or has the written consent of his or her parents.

For many years it has been the practice for eloping couples under age, to race over the border from England and to establish residential qualifications in Scotland where the age of consent is only 16. But the days when it was possible to marry legally at any time of the day, in any place at all, including over the Blacksmith's anvil at Gretna Green, by making a declaration in front of witnesses, have passed into history. Marriages today must take place before a minister of religion or a Registrar.

Scotland is still popular with elopers because of the low age of consent and Gretna Green continues to welcome more than 400 couples a year. This village is only a few miles north of Carlisle and about a mile over the border. The village thrives on the marriage business; it has motels, hotels, boarding houses, restaurants, snack bars, souvenir shops and during the summer, tourists haunt the streets and public places with cameras at the ready to snap unwary young elopers.

So famous is it that couples flock to Gretna Green from England and Wales and most parts of the continent, and amongst the youngsters waiting there for the necessary sojourn to establish residential qualifications, almost every continental language is spoken. Nor has it dawned on most of those who hide there so anxiously from irate parents, that the same laws apply throughout Scotland.

If either of the parties from south of the border happens to have a parent normally resident in Scotland, that parent's address will suffice as being the residence in Scotland of the son or daughter concerned.

CHAPTER FIVE

THE MARRIAGE OF DIVORCED PERSONS

Church of England. The Church of England expressly forbids the remarriage of a divorced person during the lifetime of a previous partner.

A clergyman has the legal right to refuse to marry in church, anyone whose previous partner is still alive, irrespective of whether the person concerned is the injured or the guilty party.

Nor can he be compelled to permit such a marriage to take place in his church. Nor can he be compelled to conduct a service for anyone who has remarried under civil law. Not all clergymen refuse however.

But it is not reasonable to refuse a clergyman permission to pray for the person concerned and, in fact, it might be possible to persuade a minister to hold a service of prayer on his or her behalf and that of the new partner. But such a service will in no sense purport to bless a remarriage and will be of a strictly private nature.

Roman Catholic Church. The Church of Rome recognizes the right of no lay authority to dissolve a marriage. In consequence there can be no "remarriage" where there is a partner surviving.

If, however, a Catholic was previously married outside the authority of the Roman Catholic Church, that body will refuse to recognize it. In such case the Church will be prepared to "marry" that person – provided of course that he or she has the legal right in civil law; by being divorced by the state from their original partner.

Free Churches. The question of the remarriage of a divorced person is very much at the discretion of each particular minister. Some of them are adamant that the original contract is binding for life, others may accept the fact that the wronged party is being unjustly penalized and yet others will consider that everyone is entitled to another chance.

In consequence an approach to a minister is necessary – and some couples have been known to "shop around" until they have found one who is sufficiently compliant.

The Society of Friends. Though Quakers believe in the sanctity of marriage, they are often prepared to accept a divorce as a necessary separation.

Nevertheless, they are not willing to consider the question of remarriage without all the circumstances being taken into account. The Monthly Meeting would need to be satisfied that the person seeking their blessing was known to them and to be of good repute. It is possible that the matter might be investigated by a small

57

committee so that the Monthly Meeting might be advised by them without the need to air all the circumstances in public.

The Monthly Meeting can be expected to authorize the remarriage within the sect, so long as they decide that the party concerned warrants their sympathy and is genuinely anxious to remarry within the Christian faith.

Civil Remarriages. The law of England and Wales recognizes a divorced person as single so long as they can produce a decree absolute. Having produced that document, a remarriage in a Registry Office is conducted on exactly the same conditions as those applying to a first marriage.

Scottish divorced persons. The only difference between the various regulations and conditions applying to remarriage, between England and Wales, and Scotland, concern the method of divorce.

In England and Wales a decree *nisi* pronounces the divorce, but neither party is free to remarry until a decree absolute has been obtained. This is obtainable on application by the successful petitioner, six weeks after the decree *nisi*.

In Scotland there is no such thing as a preliminary pronouncement. The decree is absolute from the moment of the divorce, leaving the divorced persons free to take immediate steps towards remarriage if they should so desire.

58

CHAPTER SIX

OTHER ARRANGEMENTS YOU MUST MAKE

IN the previous chapters the couple will have discovered the procedures by which their marriage may be conducted – and have decided on the one most appropriate and suitable to themselves. And of course, all other arrangements must depend on the time, the date and the venue of the marriage itself.

The date needs a lot of care in the choosing. In the first place it must coincide with available dates and times at the church where the wedding is to take place, and of course, with the convenience of the minister who will conduct the service.

And in some areas it is difficult to book the arrangements because of the demand by other couples. Saturdays, for instance, are generally reserved for weeks and even months ahead – as week-ends are usually the most convenient times for the majority of guests.

The bridegroom's normal holidays from work – and those of the bride as often as not – usually need to coincide with the honeymoon. Which suggests that the summer months is a busy time for weddings. Easter, Whitsuntide and August Bank Holidays are popular periods too, and cause queues of wedding parties at churches and registry offices up and down the land.

In any event there should be as little haste between the decision to marry and the service itself, as possible. Other arrangements might prove just as difficult to conclude, unless there is time in hand.

But once the time and the date of the wedding have been fixed, the bride and groom – and indeed, the bride's parents – can turn their attention to all the other arrangements that are so necessary to maintain the traditions and to make a complete success of the occasion.

The bridegroom is least concerned in the making of the arrangements; though he can expect to be consulted by the bride on many matters, and to have to discuss with her some of his own plans.

The honeymoon, for instance; though he will be expected to make all the arrangements for it, obviously his bride will want some say in the plans themselves.

Broadly, the bridegroom's tasks cover:

The selection of his Best Man, groomsmen and ushers.

His "bachelor party".

The purchase of the wedding ring.

The planning and booking of everything in connection with the honeymoon – not forgetting passports when needed, and the car from the reception to the station or airport if they are to leave by train or air.

Attend to buying or hiring his own wedding clothes.

The bride's list is much more complicated, though

the responsibility for most of the items will rest on the shoulders of her parents.

She must:

Complete the arrangements for the wedding service, including the church decorations, the music and the Order of Service.

Select her Chief Bridesmaid, the bridesmaids and perhaps pages, and choose their dresses.

The reception, including the venue, the menu and the wines.

The wedding cake.

The flowers and bouquets.

The wedding cars to the church and to the reception afterwards.

The invitations and press announcements.

The photographer.

Arrangements for the display of their wedding presents.

Not to mention:

Her wedding gown and all that goes with it.

Her trousseau.

Her going away outfit.

And her luggage.

Apart from the need for consultation concerning plans and arrangements, there must be some discussion concerning the payment of the bills in connection with the wedding. Everything from the decorations to the hire of the cars, the wedding breakfast and the wines, the bridesmaids' dresses, the bouquets, the photographs and even the organists' fees must be met either with a cheque or in cash.

It is usual, but by no means mandatory, for the bride's parents to pay for the reception, the cake and everything concerning the celebration after the service, while the groom meets the cost of the wedding itself and the honeymoon afterwards.

Naturally, the scale of the marriage and its celebration afterwards must be related to the financial status of those concerned – and where the resources of the parents vary considerably, it is usual for the better situated to pay a full measure towards the event.

The cost to the bride's parents can be considerable and the bridegroom's parents should bear in mind that generally their own share is trivial in comparison.

Account must be taken too, of what funds are to be held back to help the young couple to start their new life together.

Of course many a bride is insistent that the wedding day is the high-spot in her life, never to be repeated, and she expects it to be treated as such – and if there is anything to spare after the celebration, maybe she wants the honeymoon to be the talking point of her memories for the rest of her life.

Men are more inclined to favour less publicity and pageantry than their brides, but they are often in collusion with her concerning the scope of their honeymoon.

Other couples view the future rather differently.

They realize that a large sum spent on a single day's ceremonies and jollifications plus perhaps a similar sum on a fortnight's honeymoon on the continent, might be put to more practical and permanent use. A larger down-payment on their home perhaps, less furniture on the H.P. for instance, maybe more elaborate decorations and carpeting in their new house, even a little car that might have had to wait for a couple of years – and possibly, as a background to his career in business.

The Guest List

Another feature that may require careful thought is the problem of the guest list for the wedding and the reception afterwards. Of course the matter presents few problems where neither families have many relations or friends who could expect to be invited, but in some families, the numbers may well run into scores – and even then, a little forgetfulness may result in offence being taken where it was not intended.

Other couples may find that their families have a very unbalanced list of friends and relations they wish to invite to the wedding, resulting in the need for a lot of tact, common sense and maybe a certain amount of generosity.

All these problems need to be solved and minds must be made up quickly, if there isn't a great deal of time to spare. Not only will there be a waiting list for available times and dates at the church or the registry office, but almost everything else connected with a wedding is in equally urgent demand.

With holidays being booked nearly six months in advance, honeymoon reservations require equally early consideration – and attention. The printing of invitation cards can rarely be promised under a week or two, dressmaking takes a lot of time and patience and even the wedding cake needs care if it is to be as nice as the bride would like it to be.

The photographer will have a long list of appointments, so will the car hire firm, the florist; the reception rooms are likely to be spoken for on many dates, the guests may have prior appointments – and even the hairdresser may not be available at the time required, unless she is given adequate notice.

Most of the items listed above are dealt with in subsequent chapters, but it is well that all concerned should realize the amount of organization that is going to be necessary if the wedding is to be the happy day it should be.

CHAPTER SEVEN

THE BACHELOR PARTY

It has long been the custom for the prospective bride-groom to entertain his bachelor friends at a party on the night before his wedding – and as you can imagine, such affairs are generally regarded with a tolerant eye, by the older folk, as being a last wild fling before the responsibilities of matrimony descend on the young man's shoulders.

But too often, the effect on the guests; particularly on the bridegroom and the best man; has been carried over to the day of the wedding.

More than once in the past, because of the previous night's bachelor party, has a bridegroom been con-ducted to the altar by his friends, hardly fit to stand alone – and certainly not sufficiently in command of his senses to be able to follow the service in detail, or to make his vows in a proper spirit.

Many a bride has found herself alone on her wedding night while her husband slept off the hangover from his bachelor party – made worse by the "hairs of a biting dog" thrust upon him at the reception by his devoted, but sadly misguided friends.

Probably, with such unfortunate results in mind, it

has of recent years become the practice for most prospective bridegrooms to hold their bachelor parties some days in advance of the wedding, instead of on the night before it, leaving time for the after-effects to wear off and for the last minute arrangements for the wedding to be dealt with in an atmosphere of eager sobriety.

A bachelor party is usually an informal affair, held in a hotel, a restaurant or even in a night club – but whenever possible, a private room should be engaged, so that other guests of the establishment will neither be inconvenienced or diverted by the noisy conversation that is almost certain to arise.

Of course the number of guests invited to the party will be related to the number of bachelor friends the bridegroom can claim – and to the amount of money he has to spare for the occasion. The latter point must also be taken into consideration when deciding on the venue, the menu and the wines – and, in special circumstances, the entertainment to be provided.

Among the invited guests will be the brothers of both the bride and the groom, providing, of course, that they are old enough. It is generally accepted that 17 is the lower age limit, though 18 is more realistic in view of the Liquor Licensing Laws which prohibits the supplying of alcoholic beverages to anyone below that magic age.

Formal invitations are quite unnecessary; a phone call or a verbal invitation when the bridegroom happens to meet his friends, is sufficient. Dinner jackets may be worn – if all the guests either possess one, or can afford to hire one. However, formal dress is much less common nowadays.

The bridegroom is expected to arrive first at the venue for his party, in company with, or followed almost at once by his best man. This allows the groom to greet his guests as they arrive while the best man dispenses, or suggests the first round of drinks.

Of course there will be no ladies among the guests and traditionally the party is restricted to unmarried men; however, on occasion, married brothers of the groom have been included – and as it is the bridegroom's party, who can deny him the right to stretch convention a little?

The whole affair is traditionally ignored by the bride, treated with amused though shy interest by the sisters of the couple and girls of their age group, and with delighted laughter by the male relatives of an older generation, as they recall their own bachelor parties!

Usually the guests are greeted by their host in an anteroom to the private dining-room, where a table of drinks is the main attraction. One or more waiters should be in attendance – but no waitresses.

If it is impracticable to have a separate reception room, it is quite proper to have the drinks table in a corner of the private dining-room.

The drinks on show should include, besides whisky,

gin, and other short drinks and the sodas, tonics etc., that go with them, an adequate supply of bottled beers, lagers and, of course, cordials. Sometimes the caterer will make arrangements for the supply of draught beers; a highly desirable state of affairs when so many young men are having a party.

By arrangement with the caterer when booking the room and the dinner, it is possible to have these drinks charged by the tots of spirits consumed and the bottles of beer opened. This is a big advantage unless the host is prepared to either limit the supply and range of drinks available to his guests, or to pay for a number of bottles that have been barely used.

Spirits are costly today and if the selection of drinks is to be at all varied, there must inevitably be an expensive array of part-empty bottles left over after the party. Nor is it exactly dignified for the host to carry crates of unopened beer bottles to his car, after the last of his guests have gone.

Two drinks per head should suffice before moving into the dining-room. If the service is expert in the ante-room and the host alive to when he should call his guests to the table, delays and difficulties with the staff will be avoided. No objection should be taken to guests carrying their drinks to the table with them, and in this manner the meal should be served hot and on time – and any budding arguments nipped in the bud.

The design of the dinner table depends very much on

the number of guests who are to attend the party – and the shape and size of the room at their disposal.

A single, round table is the most attractive form of seating, but few hotels or restaurants possess a private dining-room of the correct dimensions where more than a dozen people can be seated in comfort.

There must be adequate room for service all around the table, yet the room must not be so extensive that the guests get the feeling that they have been abandoned in the corner of a vast, barren barn.

For fifteen guests, a round table of about 38 feet in circumference would be required – about 12 feet in diameter. The room itself could not be less than 15 feet in width and at least 20 feet in length to enable service tables to be placed conveniently in the room.

Twenty guests would probably call for a single, long table; the host seated at the top and his best man at the foot, leaving room for nine on each side.

Numbers in excess of twenty would call for a top table and two legs in the form of an inverted U. The lengths of the top table and the two legs would, of course, depend on the numbers to be seated – allowing for about 2½ feet per person as the minimum elbow room.

The host would of course sit in the middle of the top table and his best man at the foot of one of the legs. If the numbers are below about thirty, the inside of the tables should not be used – so that no one would have their backs to others.

Where numbers do exceed about thirty, it is generally not feasible to continue using the outside of the tables only. The space required would be too great and the guests too scattered either for comfort, appearance, service or conversation. Even then, though the inside of the two legs should be used, the inside of the top table should be left clear – so that everone can see his host, and he can see his guests.

The question of table decorations can well be left to the good taste of the caterer. As no ladies will be present, flowers are of minor importance; leaving the display of gleaming silver, glass and china to set off the table.

Suggestions for menus and wines are given in Chapter 15, though the caterer will advise on seasons, wines and charges to be expected.

Only two speeches are called for - though others may follow according to the humour and the inventiveness of the guests. They should be made as soon as the waiters have cleared the tables, except for coffee cups, liqueur glasses and ash trays.

The first of the speeches should come from the best man, who can be expected to speak humorously and perhaps mock-lugubriously of the fond farewell they must make to yet another deserter from the happy ranks of the unattached males – another bachelor who has succumbed to feminine wiles, and who is about to embark upon the stormy seas of matrimony. A man who was once a man, but who is now to be shackled to a washing machine and a woman's apron strings. A being who is to be forbidden the comfort of an evening pint of the best at the local and rationed to a once weekly half pint of the cheapest brew – unless accompanied by his wife.

The Best Man may make use of some further points in his speech based on his personal knowledge of the Groom.

An event or two during their schooldays.

The girls – unnamed – whom he is about to abandon.

How the cunning witch laid the trap to ensnare him.

The usual penny bun costing two pence in future.

The expense of milk – when the time comes.

The various means of escaping his fate; the river, the gas oven, or perhaps murder with a long sojourn on Dartmoor to follow.

This is the occasion for the Best Man to show his wit – and if he is wise, he will prepare for the event with all the care and secret rehearsal of a prima donna. The speech should not be too long; a good dinner and a few drinks will mellow the listeners, but make them outspoken if they get bored.

The Bridegroom responds with an equally farcical farewell to his bachelor friends – friends whom he is glad to abandon because of their shockingly selfish way of life; a bunch of reprobates, boozers and ill-mannered oafs. How he is about to enjoy the salubrious company of somebody who will cook for him, warm his slippers by the fire, sew his buttons on and wash the car for him. Somebody who will pander to his merest whim. The warm fire he will enjoy while his erstwhile friends are tramping the rain-drenched streets in search of company.

The Bridegroom can extend his speech, always in a humorous vein, to bring in:

A sad farewell to his past girl friends.

A welcome at his home for all his men friends – so long as they wipe their shoes on the doormat.

A request that financial aid should not be withheld if they ever again meet in a pub.

And a final request that they should all behave themselves at the wedding and the reception afterwards, and not disgrace him in front of his bride and his newfound relatives.

If there is to be an entertainment, it should be confined to a single act. Perhaps a cross-talk comedian, a ventriloquist, or perhaps a pianist to lead them all into a few of the tap-room ballads which are likely to suit the humour of such an occasion.

There should be no delay in getting the artist on the stand. By ten o'clock the guests will have had about a couple of hours of food and drink – and yet more drink. They will be verging on the noisy and soon after ten, they are likely to become too talkative to listen to a performer with either the attention the act deserves or the decorum that is the essence of good manners.

It is a matter of courtesy to offer the entertainer a drink after he has concluded his act – but it is not proper that he should be offered a series of drinks, until he is unable to escape and has, not necessarily willingly, to become one of the party.

On occasion, a female entertainer is engaged for this spot in the evening – but it can lead to a good deal of ill-feeling among girl friends afterwards, to a certain amount of malicious gossip and to ill-feeling when she is invited to drink with the guests.

The host and the best man should be capable of bringing the party to an end when everybody has had a thoroughly good time, but before spirits become either too boisterous or minds too fuddled. Eleven o'clock is usually quite late enough – and the wise guest will then go home either by bus or by taxi.

The host will be the last to leave – after he has made sure that every one of his guests have left and have some means of transport to their own homes.

CHAPTER EIGHT

WHO DOES WHAT?

ONE of the earliest tasks of the bride and the bride-groom is to choose those who are to be their aides, before, during and immediately after their wedding.

The matter needs careful thought if jealousies are not to be aroused. Relations often feel that they have a claim to be more than guests at a wedding; long-standing friends expect similar privileges – and not one of them may be suited to the particular duties involved.

Possibly he who considers himself most entitled to the office of best man is debarred because he has too little time to spare before the wedding, perhaps because he knows so very few of the people concerned and would, in consequence, make a poor marshal, and not improbably because, however sincere he may be, he may lack the flair for organization, the capacity to take charge of a situation, or be quick-witted enough to deal with an emergency.

Equally, an "anxious-to-be" bridesmaid may not easily be led to understand that she is the "one-too-many" of the girls who can hope to be invited to join the bridal procession. Maybe too, her lack of composure would be likely to cause embarrassment during the ceremony, or possibly she has been excluded because her ability to remain standing on her feet throughout the service is in doubt – or even because her height just cannot be matched to that of any other suitable girl.

Others, of course, have duties which are inescapable or at best, are difficult to farm out onto others. The need for the bride's father to be present at the church to give her away, for instance, is almost obligatory. Only where he is either dead or physically incapable of attending the service, should a deputy be appointed.

The Chief Bridesmaid

It is quite usual for the bride to seek the help of her eldest unmarried sister as her chief bridesmaid, or, if she has no such sister, her best unmarried friend.

There is no bounden duty laid on the bride to make such a choice if she considers another unmarried relative or friend temperamentally more suitable – but the alternative selection should not be made lightly and the unmarried sister or best friend who has been passed over, should be told by the bride herself, the reason for her decision, in the hope that goodwill and harmony will not be jeopardized.

The chief bridesmaid's duties are concerned mainly with two things; personal attention to the bride and the marshalling of the bridesmaids and pages.

She might be expected to help the bride to choose the bridesmaids' dresses, to rehearse them in their duties and to take charge of the bride's impedimenta of gloves and bouquet during the service.

She might be called upon to help dress the bride for her wedding, though this task is usually claimed by the bride's mother as a last service to her daughter. In any event, the chief bridesmaid will have enough to do to dress herself and to see to it that the bridesmaids are properly arrayed for the occasion; their headdresses, their bouquets, their shoes and the correct hang of their gowns – not to mention their arrival at the church well in advance of the bride.

During the service, the chief bridesmaid's station is immediately behind the bride and the bride's father. She will follow them in procession to the chancel steps and then, passing her own bouquet to the nearest bridesmaid, she will take the bridal bouquet. She draws the bride's veil clear of her face when it is time for her to make her responses and takes charge of her gloves while the bridegroom places the ring on the bride's finger.

When the newly wed couple follow the minister into the vestry for the formality of signing the register, she and the best man follow immediately behind them.

Often, the chief bridesmaid and the best man are chosen to sign the register as witnesses of the marriage.

The chief bridesmaid should be available to the bride during the reception, to smooth away any little worries or difficulties that may arise – often in consultation with the best man. And her final duty is to help the bride into her "going away" outfit and to see her to her car.

The Bridesmaids

The bridesmaids are chosen by the bride from amongst her young relatives and friends – not forgetting those of the bridegroom. They generally number two or four, though for important weddings the numbers may rise as high as six or even eight. They need not all be girls; two young boys as pages may be included. Pages are always very young; 5 to 8 years of age being the most acceptable limits – though there is nothing mandatory about it. They are nearly always young brothers of the couple, or nephews.

The bride almost always tries to match the couples for sizes, sometimes a difficult task but making a most attractive picture when she has been successful. It is the bride's prerogative too, to choose the bridesmaid's dresses – and the pages uniforms. This includes hats, slippers – in fact, the whole of the ensemble.

By tradition, the mothers of the bridesmaids each pay for their daughters attire – an expensive business if the bride's choice happens to be ambitious. And, of course, if the dresses are too resplendent, they might prove to be of little use to the young ladies afterwards.

Because of the burden on the parents, it is a matter for the bride to take care not to invite anyone to act as her bridesmaid whose parents would be unlikely to welcome the expense – or, as is very often the case today, the bride's parents provide the whole of the ensemble for each of the bridesmaids.

Whoever pays for the dresses and the accessories, it

is usual to allow the bridesmaids to keep them after the wedding. In any event, it would seem improbable that the dresses would fit anyone else – or because of the style, be worth preserving!

A good dressmaker should prove of immense help in designing the ensemble; she will advise too, on what is suitable for the time of the year, the fashionable styles and have a sense of matching colours, and of trimmings that will enhance rather than detract from the bridal outfit.

She will be able to make suggestions concerning the modern trend in headdresses; be that hats, haloes, tiaras or bows. She will know too, whether or not veils should be worn by the bridesmaids – and even be able to advise on the most suitable bouquets to match or contrast with the gowns.

The duties of the bridesmaids and pages are to assist the bride from the moment she arrives at the church for her wedding until she finally leaves the reception on the first stage of her honeymoon.

"Assist" is hardly the word as far as the wedding ceremony is concerned; the bridesmaids and pages are merely decorative in the procession and have no other duties then tending the bridal train – if it should be long enough to require attention.

In the procession they follow in pairs behind the bride, the pages leading and the taller or older bridesmaids coming last.

At the reception afterwards, the bridesmaids might

be expected to carry around the portions of the wedding cake at the proper time, and offer them to the guests – but after that, their duties are complete and they can enjoy themselves for the rest of the day as each of them sees fit.

Matron of Honour

There is no absolute need for a bride to be attended by a retinue of bridesmaids. Sometimes it may be that she has no young female relatives or indeed, any suitable young friends available. This often happens if the bride is new to the district, or has travelled some considerable distance to marry.

Sometimes too, the bride may be older than that of the average bride where young bridesmaids may seem to her to be out of place; or it may even be that she is most anxious to ask some particular woman to attend her who happens to be married.

In all such cases it is quite usual and even fashionable for the bride to be attended by a matron of honour. The lady chosen will be a married woman and she will be the only attendant, acting as the chief – and only – bridesmaid.

Her duties are identical with those of a chief bridesmaid, but she will not wear the finery of one. Generally, she will wear an afternoon gown with, of course, a hat.

In such cases the bride too, usually abandons the full wedding dress and veil for an outfit similar to that worn by her matron of honour – though this is by no means a must.

The Bride's Mother

The bride's mother is one of those who have inescapable duties to perform in connection with her daughter's wedding – unless of course, she happens to be incapacitated through illness, when her mantle will fall on the bride's eldest sister if she has one, or on an aunt or even a grandmother.

Yet, despite the fact that she will probably have to work harder than anyone else to make for the success of the occasion, the bride's mother will have almost no official part in the wedding itself.

She will carry the whole of the responsibility for the social side of the event and as the hostess she will issue the invitations to the wedding guests both to the ceremony and to the reception afterwards. She will need to exercise a great deal of tact, too, to include as far as possible, the guests suggested by the bridegroom's parents, bearing in mind that her husband will be expected to pay the bills!

The bride's mother will, no doubt, be deeply concerned in helping to choose the bridal gown and no doubt her advice will be sought concerning the bridesmaids' dresses.

Among the other cares she must shoulder are:

1. The printing and dispatching of the invitations.

2. The press announcements.

3. The printing of the Order of Service as arranged between the couple and the minister.

4. The church decorations.

5. The wedding bouquets – in consultation with the bride and her dressmaker, to make sure that they are in harmony with the *tout ensemble*.

6. Ordering the wedding cars to take the bride and bridesmaids, and of course herself, to the service. She will need to order too, cars wanted by other guests – and to take everybody from the church to the reception afterwards. The only cars, other than those privately owned, that will not require her attention, are those that will carry the bridegroom and his best man to the church – and the "going away" car for the bridal couple on the first stage of their honeymoon.

7. The wedding cake and the arrangements for its delivery to the hotel or restaurant where the reception is to be held.

8. The photographer – usually outside the church immediately after the service, if the weather is fine and summery. Alternatively, the official party must call at the photographers on their journey from the church to the reception – or preferably arrange for a room to be set aside at the scene of the reception for the use of the photographer. This latter suggestion is particularly

desirable as the photographer will need to be present at the reception to photograph the cutting of the cake.

9. Arranging the details of the reception in consultation with the manager or caterer of the establishment where this is to be held, including:

(a) The seating arrangements.

(b) Drawing up the table plan and the printing of place-cards.

(c) The menu.

(d) The wines.

(e) The table decorations.

(f) The purchase of privately printed table napkins – if this is desired.

(g) Booking a private room for the bride where she can change into her "going away" outfit.

10. The collection of what is left of the wedding cake after the reception; the cutting and boxing of the portions for posting to distant relatives and friends.

As the wedding, in all probability, will take place in the district where the bride lives, her mother can expect to have to do some entertaining, in addition to the gathering of their friends and relatives at the reception. This will be particularly strenuous if the bridegroom, his family and friends come from any considerable distance.

As the hostess, the bride's mother may find herself

involved in arranging hotel accommodation for some of her guests and may even feel duty bound to put some of the bridegroom's relatives up in her own home.

She will also find that her daughter will need her help in dressing for the wedding and though it is the duty of the chief bridesmaid to attend the bride, few mothers are willing to forego this last chore for their daughters.

She will then leave the bride at home with her father and make haste, probably alone, to reach the church ahead of her.

Her place during the marriage service is in the front row of pews, among her other children and perhaps her parents; on the bride's side of the aisle, to the left facing the altar.

She takes no part in the service until she is led by the bridegroom's father to the vestry to witness the final scene; the signing of the marriage register.

She and her husband then leave the church immediately after the newlyweds. They are the hosts at the reception and must of course, be there first, in time to receive their guests.

The Bride's Father

The bride's father has the dual privilege of giving his daughter away at her wedding – and paying for the reception afterwards.

Dressed in a morning coat, grey trousers, cravat and a grey top hat – and wearing a white buttonhole similar to that worn by the bridegroom and the best man – the bride's father escorts his daughter from their home to the church. If her father should happen to be dead or physcially incapable of attending the wedding, the bride's eldest brother or male guardian, or uncle takes his place.

He arrives at the church with the bride on his arm after everyone else has gathered within – though it is bad form to keep the minister and the congregation waiting after the appointed time. Almost at once, with his daughter on his right arm, he will lead the procession towards the chancel steps.

At the proper time in the service, he will take his daughter's hand and give it to the priest in a gesture of giving her away.

After the service, the bride's father accompanies the bridegroom's mother into the vestry in the wake of the newlyweds, to see the final act of the marriage – the signing of the register.

Immediately after leaving the church, he will hurry with his wife to the venue of the reception where, as host and hostess, they greet their guests.

Finally, the bride's father may be called on by the best man, during the reception, to propose the toast of the "Bride and Bridegroom".

The Best Man

The best man is chosen by the bridegroom from amongst his relatives or friends who are still unmarried, and generally, it is his closest companion that is honoured.

The duties are onerous and the bridegroom would be well advised to make his selection with extreme care. The best man will find himself a sort of master of ceremonies, the chief usher, the repository of valuables – such as the wedding ring and the certificate permitting the marriage, organizer-in-chief, toastmaster and paymaster. He is also likely to find himself the bridegroom's messenger boy, father confessor, persuader, remembrancer, office boy and valet.

Obviously he must have a flair for organization, a steady nerve, be a good mixer and have limitless tact.

His many duties include:

1. Taking the bridegroom to his wedding – on time.

2. Detailing the ushers to their duties.

3. Safeguarding the wedding ring until it is to be placed on the bride's finger.

4. After the service, accompanying the chief bridesmaid to the vestry, behind the bride and bridegroom. He and the chief bridesmaid are usually chosen as the two witnesses to sign the register – though this is not obligatory. Under the circumstances and to avoid confusion at the very last moment, it is well for the bride and the bridegroom to decide and arrange, well in advance, who the official witnesses are to be.

5. He is almost the last person to leave the vestry

and yet is expected to be the first at the church door to usher the newlyweds to their places in front of the photographer and then to see them to their car for the journey to the reception. He then ushers the guests into their cars in turn – parents first, grandparents, uncles and aunts, bridesmaids and then the friends and more distant relatives.

6. He pays the marriage fees to the minister, the verger and the organist, including the choir if this has been agreed in advance.

7. At the reception he calls on the speakers and replies to the toast of "The Bridesmaids" on their behalf.

8. He reads out the telegrams of congratulation that have been received.

9. He sees the couple into their car after the reception, ready for the start of their honeymoon journey, and hands over the various documents such as rail, air or steamer tickets, passports and route maps, which he has been safeguarding nervously during the ceremony and the reception.

Other responsibilities include:

(a) the hire of the car which takes he and the bridegroom to the church – and the "going away" car or taxi for the newlyweds.

(b) act as baggage master to the couple.

Though the best man is supposed to help the bridegroom to dress for his wedding, this is hardly necessary with modern clothes. In the picturesque days of the Prince Regent, of course, with the magnificent velvets, silks and satins worn by bridegrooms; stocks, stockings and shoe buckles; the best man needed the services of a valet to help him dress the nervous buck – and many an hour to spare for the purpose.

Today, the best man usually arrives at the bride-grooms' home as he is dressing: collects the certificate, the wedding ring, identifies the baggage, takes charge of the keys, the various tickets and other documents needed for the honeymoon and the cash necessary to pay the marriage fees at the church – a nerve-wracking business, if nothing is to be forgotten – and even then he will probably find that the nervous bridegroom has neglected to provide himself with a pair of black socks or has broken a shoelace and there isn't a spare!

The best man usually produces the buttonholes for the bridegroom and himself, watches the clock and worries about the taxi arriving on time. Nothing could make a more embarrassing start to a wedding than for the bridegroom to arrive at the church after his bride!

And from there on he continually fingers the ring in his waistcoat pocket, knowing that though he would be by no means the first best man to forget it, his failure to produce it at the right moment might almost constitute a disaster.

The best man's clothes are similar to those worn by

the bridegroom. A morning coat, grey trousers and grey tie – though if the wedding is less formal, both might wear dark lounge suits with propriety. Button-holes will be white and similar to those worn by the bridegroom and all other male members of the official party – whether dressed in morning coats or lounge suits.

Ushers

The ushers are chosen by the bridegroom, generally in consultation with his best man, from amongst the unmarried brothers and friends of his own, and of his bride.

Two are sufficient – unless there is a very long list of guests to be seated in the church.

The ushers must, of course, arrive first at the church and as the guests appear, they hand them their Order of Service sheets and conduct them to their seats. Relatives and friends of the bride sit in the pews on the left of the aisle facing the chancel steps, and those of the bridegroom, on the right – the immediate families of the bride and bridegroom being placed in the front pews on their respective sides of the aisle.

Obviously, it is better to choose ushers who know most of the guests and who will have less need to ask them if they are "friends of the bride or the bride-groom?"

Dress for the ushers should be similar to that worn

by the bridegroom and the best man; usually morning coats, grey trousers and a wedding tie. White button-holes, usually of carnations, are worn in their coat lapels, matching those of the bridegroom and the best man.

Moss Bros., of Covent Garden, London w.c.2, are renowned for their hire service in wedding clothes for men and women. They have branches throughout Britain and they also do a postal service from London.

CHAPTER NINE

ANNOUNCEMENTS AND SENDING OUT THE INVITATIONS

THE first public proclamation of the forthcoming wedding is made at the time of the engagement of the couple. Such announcements receive much less attention than they did some years ago, and in fact, there is no longer any absolute need to have the event published in the press at all.

However, there are occasions when an announcement in the advertisement columns of the press is of value to the newly engaged couple – particularly to those who have a very wide circle of friends and acquaintances. In such instances it might well be impracticable to write a letter to every one of them.

Sometimes, too, it might be that one or other of the couple happens to be a figure of either national importance or of wide public interest – a politician or a pop-singer, perhaps – making the announcement a matter of public concern. Any such announcements, of course, would be enough to bring the reporters and photographers flocking to the door, on the instant!

In such cases, and where friends and relatives of the couple are widely scattered over the country, the announcements should be made in one or more of the national daily newspapers, where a wide circulation is assured. *The Times,* the *Daily Telegraph* and the *Guardian,* the *Scotsman* and *Glasgow Herald* are five which spring to mind at once, as publishing special announcement columns.

If it happens. however, that the friends and relatives are fairly tightly domiciled in a single large city or county, the local newspaper is the best medium – and, of course, is considerably less expensive in which to advertise than in the national morning newspapers. If the bride and bridegroom do happen to live in districts distant from one another, it might be wise to use the press of each locality in which to proclaim the betrothal and the forthcoming wedding.

The advertisement should be sent to the Classified Advertisements Manager of the newspapers concerned, and they should be drafted in the following manner:

HIMSELF : HERSELF

An engagement is announced and a marriage will shortly take place, between Peter John Himself, only son of Mr. and Mrs. G. H. Himself of The Towers, Esher Meade, and Ann, younger daughter of Col. and Mrs. L. R. Herself of 12 Fir Tree Lane, Woodhouse, Northumberland.

It could be varied to read:

HIMSELF : HERSELF

An engagement is announced between Peter,

only son of Mr. and Mrs. G. H. Himself of The Towers, Esher Meade, and Ann, younger daughter of Col. and Mrs. L. R. Herself of 12 Fir Tree Lane, Woodhouse, Northumberland.

If, however, the bridegroom bears a title or carries a military rank, the wording of the advertisement would more probably be as follows:

HIMSELF : HERSELF

An engagement is announced between Flight Lieutenant Peter John Himself, A.F.C., R.A.F., only son of Mr. and Mrs. G. H. Himself of The Towers, Esher Meade, and Ann, younger daughter of Col. and Mrs. L. R. Herself of 12 Fir Tree Lane, Woodhouse, Northumberland.

If it should be that the bride's father is dead, the last sentence of the announcement should read:

. . . and Ann, younger daughter of the late Col. L. R. Herself and Mrs. Herself of 12 Fir Tree Lane . . .

If it is the bride's mother who has died, the sentence will read:

. . . and Ann, younger daughter of Col. L. R. Herself and the late Mrs. Herself of 12 Fir Tree Lane . . .

If the bride's parents have been divorced, the address of each of them should be given, as follows:

. . . and Ann, younger daughter of Col. L. R.
Herself of 12 Fir Tree Lane, Woodhouse, North-
umberland, and Mrs. R. L. Herself of The Hall,
Willingdon.

If the parents have been divorced and the bride's mother has remarried, the advertisement should conclude:

. . . and Ann, younger daughter of Col. L. R.
Herself of 12 Fir Tree Lane, Woodhouse, North-
umberland, and Mrs. C. B. Bodkin of 49 The
Grove, Coldharbour.

If it is the bridegroom's parents who are either dead
or have been divorced, precisely the same amendment
to the announcement should be made in the first sentence, as would be made in the last sentence, where the
bride was concerned.

In due course invitations to the wedding and the
reception need to be printed and dispatched by post to
those for whom they are intended. The list is a matter
for the bride's parents – as hosts, they must select their
guests. But is is common and much kinder, for the two
sets of parents and the engaged couple to consult one
another on the subject.

It is reasonable to assume that both the bride and the
bridegroom – and their parents – will wish to invite
similar numbers from amongst their own relatives and
friends – though this is not necessarily the case. For
instance, a bridegroom may come from some considerable distance to his wedding; a distance not easily

covered by all his friends. Or perhaps the bride is a member of some society which might bring her an unusually large number of friends.

In any event, the bride's people must be left to make the final decision as to numbers to be invited – at least as far as the reception is concerned; they will be expected to pay the bill for the whole of the entertainment and it could well become an embarrassing amount.

At one time it was usual to issue separate invitations to the wedding ceremony and the reception afterwards, but it is customary today to combine the invitations on a single card – unless, of course, there is to be a large discrepancy between the numbers invited to attend the ceremony and those expected to be present at the reception later.

Invitations should be sent out well in advance of the event; probably as much as six weeks before the wedding, so as to give the guests plenty of time to complete their own arrangements and to decline any alternative invitations they may receive to other functions on the same day and at the same time.

The invitations may be sent out in the form of *pro forma* cards; printed in a standard fashion, leaving the sender to fill in the names and addresses in the appropriate places.

These can be seen at any good stationers or printers, but it will be found that especially printed cards will cost very little extra and in any event, be well worth the small additional expense.

A very popular format is:

> *Colonel and Mrs. Leslie R. Herself*
> *request the pleasure of the company of*
>
> ....
> *at the marriage of their daughter*
> *Ann*
> *to*
> *Mr. Peter John Himself*
> *at St. George's Parish Church, Woodhouse*
> *on Saturday April 20th 1969*
> *at 11 a.m.*
> *and at a reception afterwards at the*
> *Carlton Hotel.*

12 Fir Tree Lane
Woodhouse
Northumberland   R.S.V.P.

Of course the first line of the invitation will vary with the status of those sending the invitation.

If the bride's mother is dead, it will read:

> *Colonel Leslie R. Herself*
> *requests the pleasure . . .*

If it is the father who is dead, it will read:

> *Mrs. Leslie R. Herself*
> *requests the pleasure of . . .*

And if both parents are dead, the invitations will be issued in the names of the guardians or relatives who are to act as hosts for the occasion.

The R.S.V.P. is most necessary, as the hostess must know in advance, how many guests she may expect – especially for the meal at the reception.

Replies should be brief, dispatched without delay and couched in the third person, such as:

15 Wingrove Terrace
Ellesmere.

Mr. and Mrs. Joseph Fleet and their daughter Phyllis thank Colonel and Mrs. Leslie R. Herself for their kind invitation to their daughter's wedding at St. George's Parish Church on Saturday 20th April 1969 at 11 a.m. and to a reception afterwards at the Carlton Hotel, and are most happy to accept. 11th March 1969.

Such a note requires no signature.

If it is impossible to accept the invitation, either because of a prior engagement or for some private, family reason, it is a matter of courtesy both to acknowledge the invitation, and to make your decision not to attend, clear. Apart from the unnecessary expense borne by the bride's parents, nothing will reflect more opprobrium on yourself than for your name card to lie at a vacant place at the reception table.

The refusal should be as brief as the acceptance and similarly couched in the third person, though an excuse might be added, however vague it may appear to be:

> 15 *Wingrove Terrace*
> *Ellesmere.*

Mr. and Mrs. Joseph Fleet and their daughter Phyllis thank Colonel and Mrs. Herself for their kind invitation to their daughter's wedding at St. George's Parish Church on Saturday 20th April 1969, and to the reception afterwards.

Unfortunately they have accepted a prior engagement for that date and must therefore decline with regret.

11th March 1969.

And again, no signature is required.

There are occasions, when the invitations to the wedding outstrips the ability of the hosts to entertain at the reception afterwards. This may be because of the expense, or it may have been brought about by a recent bereavement, which has decided the bride and her parents to restrict the celebrations to a small, private gathering of the two families and perhaps a few of their close friends.

In neither case is there any need for the bride's parents to limit the numbers they invite to the church, but it is usual then, to omit all mention of the reception on the invitation cards.

Where, however, it is intended to invite a particular guest to the reception afterwards, it is possible to have extra cards printed accordingly and inserted together with the invitation to the wedding, in the same envelope.

Such cards might read:

> *Colonel and Mrs. Leslie R. Herself request the pleasure of Mr. and Mrs. Joseph Fleet and their daughter's company at a private reception to be given by them after their daughter's wedding, at the Carlton Hotel, Woodhouse on Saturday 20th April 1969.*
>
> *12 Fir Tree Lane*
> *Woodhouse*
> *Northumberland*　　　　　　　R.S.V.P.

However, such invitation cards are unusual today, unless the numbers to be invited are large, but as the obvious intention is to limit the number of guests at the reception, it is quite proper to write across the bottom of the wedding invitations of those concerned:

> *And to a small reception afterwards at the Carlton Hotel, Woodhouse.*

Sometimes an invitation already accepted must be declined, possibly because of illness, an accident, or even through a sudden death in the family. In such case the bride's parents should be informed at once. It may give them time to amend the table plan at the reception instead of having to leave an empty seat.

A simple note is all that is necessary; perhaps:

> *15 Wingrove Terrace*
> *Ellesmere.*

> *Mr. and Mrs. Fleet and their daughter Phyllis sincerely regret the necessity, because of a bereavement in the family, to have to inform you that they will now be unable to attend your daughter's wedding on 20th April 1969, or the reception afterwards.*
> *21st March 1969.*

Again, there is no need for a signature.

CHAPTER TEN

THE ENGAGEMENT RING AND THE WEDDING GIFTS

THE engagement ring is perhaps the first serious token of affection from a prospective bridegroom to his future wife, but as this is more in the nature of a seal to a contract between them, it can hardly be classed as a "present".

Other gifts from a bridegroom to his bride will obviously follow between their engagement and the wedding – but there are certain taboos that should be observed in this connection. He should not buy clothing for her nor should he buy expensive items such as jewellery or furs; nor should the bridegroom pay for any items that could suggest that he was "keeping" her.

The bride, in her turn, should not occupy any home that the bridegroom has bought or procured, in advance of the wedding; nor should she make use of any furniture, linen or any other articles that have been bought for their joint use in their new home.

It is quite usual for the bride to give her future husband an engagement present; a cigarette case is popular where this is appropriate, a pair of cuff-links was common while they were fashionable or most suitably a signet ring.

Soon after the invitations to the wedding have been sent out, presents will begin to arrive for the betrothed couple from relatives and friends. Such offerings should always be addressed to the bride at her home and not to the bridegroom – even though it may happen that the donor has never even met the bride!

The presents may vary from the decorative to the practical, from the purely personal to the "homey" and from the very expensive to the intrinsically valueless. Yet whatever the value or the nature of the gift, each will be as preciously intended as any other; each will assuredly be given as an expression of well-wishing and each probably in accordance with its donor's means.

Presents will usually turn out to be both useful and attractive, every one of them a boon to the recipients – except those that are duplicates, one of another. And in such cases the need for tact is absolutely essential, if it is going to be possible to arrange to exchange unwanted items for something more useful, without unduly offending the donor.

Of course, other, closer relatives may ask the bride to give some indication of what she would like – an invitation that may well be as embarrassing to deal with as in the case of duplicated items.

How do you answer such a request?

With the greatest care and the best will in the world, it is too easy to upset a relative by suggesting the sort of present that may well cost more that the donor intended to pay; more perhaps than he or she can readily afford to pay. Equal resentment may be caused by suggesting the sort of present that is cheap, to a relation who is able to afford something better – and likes to display the fact!

It is possible, with a little thought, however, to avoid embarrassment and yet suggest something that really is wanted, and yet be within the range of almost everyone's pocket. "Crockery" for instance, could mean anything from a six-piece tea set, to a 156-piece dinner service; "Cutlery" might suggest anything between a dozen silver tea spoons and 144 items in a truly magnificent mahogany cabinet – and of course "blankets" may suggest, a pair, or two or three complete sets of bedding.

Cheques are often more useful to a newly married couple who will have a hundred-and-one needs before they complete their home – even though the bare envelope on the display table looks very bleak and lonely. But except in the case of fathers, it is not the kind of present that can be suggested with propriety by the bride or her bridegroom.

On the night before the wedding, where arrangements can be made at the venue for the reception afterwards, a room should be set aside for the display of the wedding presents.

Such an exhibition can be made most attractive; white tablecloths and tiers of boxes underneath can do much to set off the beauty and interest of the collection of items. Each present should have a card sent with it so that it may stand beside the piece on the display tables, giving the donor's name and address. In the case of cheques, only an envelope is displayed stating the name and address of the donor but giving no information concerning its value. Under no circumstances should the cheque itself be displayed.

A similar restriction should be placed on less usual presents, such as an Insurance Policy, the deeds of a house or a shares certificate. Envelopes should represent the items on the display tables, endorsed with the words "Insurance Policy", "Deeds of House" or "Shares Certificate" – and the name and address of the donor.

Immediately after the reception the bride's parents should remove the presents to their own home, where a suitable display should again be arranged for the benefit of friends and relatives who had been unable to attend the reception. This display may well last until a few days before the end of the newly married couple's honeymoon, when her mother and father should place them in the new home ready for their daughter and son-in-law's return.

After the honeymoon it is the bride's duty to write and thank the individual donors of presents. Such letters should be sent out almost as soon as she takes up her residence in her new home, but where the numbers make the task a lengthy one, a verbal, even a telephone message will serve as an interim measure. However close the giver and however fulsome the verbal thanks, a letter in due course is obligatory.

There is a certain amount of tradition to be observed in the sending of wedding presents:

(a) Relatives should send a present whether or not they attend the reception and the wedding – so long as they have been invited.

(b) All those attending the wedding ceremony and the reception afterwards are expected to send a present.

(c) There is no need for a friend to send a present when the invitation has been declined – though it is usual to do so when the cause is illness or for some other reason that, if it had not risen, would not have meant a refusal.

(d) There is no need to send a present where the invitation is to the wedding ceremony only – and does not include the reception afterwards.

(e) All presents should be sent to the bride at her parents' home, before the wedding – where they are sent afterwards, they should be addressed to both the bride and the bridegroom at their new home.

(f) Once in a while, though rarely indeed, a present is intended for the bridegroom only. In such case it should be sent to his parents' address and be acknowledged by him after the honeymoon. It may be displayed with the other presents.

Such a present, given in such a manner, may cause a certain amount of resentment and ill-feeling unless the reason is fully understood. If it is likely to be misconstrued, it should not be sent.

(g) If a present is received, it is incumbent to invite the donor to the wedding ceremony and usually, though not necessarily, to the reception afterwards. To avoid such a happening, it is best to wait until invitations to the wedding and the reception have been received before sending presents.

It is common practice for the bridegroom to present each of the bridesmaids with a small present immediately after the wedding – probably at a quiet but convenient moment during the reception. A small, quite inexpensive piece of jewellery or a trinket is usual.

If there are any pages, they should not be overlooked – a plaything is generally most suitable.

CHAPTER ELEVEN

THE CEREMONY

Church of England

A minister of the Church of England may not refuse to perform a marriage service so long as he is sure that there is no legal or ecclesiastical objection to it – and indeed, he must satisfy himself that the law does in fact specifically permit each particular marriage.

Though the marriage may be in order under civil law, where it is forbidden by the church, no minister may celebrate it in his church – nor may he permit anyone else to perform the service. This applies in the case of the remarriage of a divorced person and takes no cognizance of the innocence or guilt of he or she wishing to be remarried.

A minister may be persuaded to bless the couple in a private ceremony, but it must not purport to be in any sense a marriage service.

Any day of the week may be chosen by the couple as their wedding day, including Sundays and even Good Fridays – though of course it is necessary for them to consult the minister concerned to make sure that it is convenient to him.

The popular days for such happy occasions are

Fridays and Saturdays, both because it probably gives the couple an extra week-end for their honeymoon and because it is generally more convenient for their guests. Saturday mornings usually result in a queue of wedding parties at most churches and those who wish to marry at such a time on that day, should talk to the minister of the church about it well in advance of the projected date. Generally months ahead.

Times preferred are between 10 a.m. and noon – leaving plenty of time for the reception afterwards and more hours of daylight for the couple's journey to their honeymoon resort.

Also well in advance, the clergyman should be consulted about the decoration of his church. White flowers and greenery are usual for weddings. Lilies, roses, carnations, chrysanthemums, and dahlias are popular – with perhaps ferns or evergreens. A vast display is quite unnecessary – and any good florist will do the whole thing for you.

A decision has to be made in advance too, concerning the music for the service and it is well to have a talk with the organist as soon as possible. Though it is accepted that it is the bride's prerogative to choose the hymns and, of course, the wedding march, it is obvious that the organist's advice should be taken fully into account.

This is particularly applicable where a choir is needed.

From this point it is possible to arrange the full

details of the service on a printed sheet, known as the "Order of Service". And if the bridal couple and the bride's mother complete all these arrangements in good time, it is possible to have the Order of Service printed for the use of all concerned.

On the morning of the wedding the excitement rises. At an early hour the bride will start dressing with her mother's help; the bridegroom will dress too, though less formally while the bridesmaids and the guests prepare less hastily in their own homes.

An hour before the wedding is due to start, the chief bridesmaid should arrive at the bride's home – dressed and all ready. She will then help the bride to finish her dressing whilst the bride's mother snatches an opportunity to don her wedding attire.

At about the same time the best man should arrive, dressed for the ceremony, at the bridegroom's home.

Also at about the same time, the bridesmaids will begin to congregate at the bride's home while the ushers make ready individually in their own homes, for the service.

At least half an hour before the ceremony is due to start, the head usher or groomsman must arrive at the church – first of all the party and the guests. Immediately afterwards the other ushers are due and should then receive their final instructions from him.

The head usher must point out to them that the guests ought to be met at the church door and conducted from there to their pews. He will remind them that the bride's mother, brothers and sisters and her grand-parents should be seated in the front pew to the left of the nave facing the altar.

Others of the bride's relatives and friends should be seated on the same side of the church in descending order of relationship and closeness of friendship – so far as is conveniently possible – from the pews im-mediately behind the bride's mother to the back of the church.

Similarly, the bridegroom's relatives and friends will occupy the pews on the right of the nave – also seating the closer members of his family, including his parents, in the front row on that side.

As a last instruction, the head usher will hand over copies of the Order of Service to the ushers, either to lay in the pews in advance, or more usually, to hand out as they conduct the wedding party and the guests to their seats.

Meanwhile, the best man should be making quite certain that the bridegroom is properly dressed for his wedding, should be checking the items he must take with him – the wedding ring in his waistcoat pocket, for instance; money in his hip pocket to pay the marriage fees, and the couple's rail, boat or air tickets, passports and hotel reservations in his inside morning coat pocket.

Twenty minutes before the service is due to start, he should conduct the bridegroom to the church and they then usually find themselves some secluded spot in which to wait.

From about now on, the guests begin to arrive and must be conducted to their seats. Those who have not met for some time and those who are meeting for the first time, will be inclined to chat at the church door, causing a little obstruction and possibly creating a hold-up when the bride arrives. A little gentle hint here and there should get them to their places in ample time, however.

The chief bridesmaid should arrive in company with the other bridesmaids and the pages, not less than five minutes before the bride is due. They should gather in the church porch ready to form a procession and again, though the guests will tend to stop and talk to them, they should be dissuaded as much as possible as time will be getting short.

At the time the bridesmaids arrive, the best man should lead the bridegroom along the nave to the chancel steps – the best man on the bridegroom's right.

The arrival, entrance and bridal procession is one of the high spots of pageantry for the occasion and it is important therefore that everybody should be in their places in good time. And the bride must arrive on her father's arm exactly on time. They arrive at the church last and in modern traffic conditions it is well for them to leave home early, even if it means that they have to cruise around for a few minutes to adjust their arrival to the exactly scheduled time.

Nor must this be an occasion when the bride exercises a woman's right to be late. It would be discourteous to the minister, the organist and the guests – and besides, it may cause serious delay to someone else's wedding which may be due to take place immediately afterwards.

The organist will be warned of the bride's arrival, and move over from the introductory music to the wedding march, and with his daughter on his right arm, her father will lead her forward into the body of the church, in slow time – the pages and the bridesmaids taking up their places in the procession, in couples with the chief bridesmaid to the left of the leading pair and just behind the bride and her father.

To effect a properly paced procession, the bride and her father should move off with the left foot in time with the march, those following picking up the step as they fall into pairs behind.

The officiating clergyman and the choir may march in slow time down the nave towards the bridal procession and then turn to precede it – or the minister may await the bride on the chancel steps.

The bridegroom and his best man should turn to welcome the bride as she approaches and her father should lead her to the bridegroom's left, so that, as they face the altar and the minister, they stand from left to right – the bride's father, the bride, the bridegroom and the best man.

Once they are in position with the bridesmaids

standing in pairs behind the bride, the chief bridesmaid should step forward to relieve the bride of her bouquet, just as her father releases her arm. She takes the bride's gloves and sets her veil clear of her face, back over her head. The chief bridesmaid then returns to her place immediately behind the bride, satisfying herself that the bridesmaids and pages are in their places too.

At this point the minister begins the wedding with the ordained service, stating the reason for the gathering in the church, the reason for matrimony, followed by a demand to know if there is any impediment to the marriage, both from the bridal couple and then from the congregation.

If he is satisfied that there is no legal objection to the union, he will then ask the man:

> "Wilt thou have this woman to thy wedded wife, to live together after God's ordinance in the holy estate of Matrimony? Wilt thou have her, comfort her, honour and keep her in sickness and in health; and forsaking all other, keep thee only unto her, so long as ye both shall live?"

The Man shall answer: "I will."

The minister then asks the woman:

> "Wilt thou have this man to thy wedded husband, to live together after God's ordinance in the holy estate of Matrimony? Wilt thou obey him, and serve him, love, honour, and keep him in sickness and

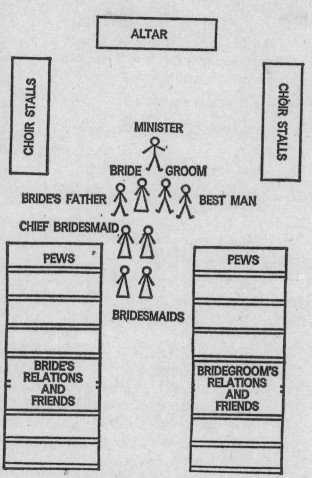

Figure 1. Positions in the Church

health; and forsaking all other, keep thee only to him, so long as ye both shall live?"

(The bride may elect to be married under the "new" service where she is not obliged to include the promise 'to obey'.)

The Woman shall answer: "I will."

The Minister will then ask:

"Who giveth this woman to be married to this Man?"

The bride's father answers: "I do."

The bride's father passes his daughter's right hand to the clergyman, palm downwards. He passes it into the right hand of the bridegroom.

The bride's father's part in the service is now ended and he may, if he wishes, drop back and take his place in the front pew beside his wife.

The bridegroom will then say after the minister:

"I . . . . take thee, ... to my wedded wife, to have and to hold from this day forward, for better for worse, in sickness and in health, to love and to cherish, till death us do part, according to God's holy ordinance; and thereto I plight thee my troth."

The pair will free their hands and then the bride will take the right hand of the man in her own right hand and say after the minister:

"I . . . . take thee . . . . to my wedded
husband, to have and to hold from this day
forward, for better for worse, for richer for poorer,
in sickness and in health, to love, cherish, and to
obey, till death us do part, according to God's
holy ordinance; and thereto I give thee my troth."

As they free their hands the best man takes the
wedding ring from his waistcoat pocket and places it
on the surface of the open Prayer Book proffered by
the minister. The minister will offer the ring to the
bridegroom who will take it and place it on the third
finger of the bride's left hand. (She should not be
wearing her engagement ring or any other ring on that
finger.)

While the bridegroom holds the ring in place, he
must repeat after the minister:

"With this ring I thee wed, with my body I
thee worship, and with all my worldly goods I
thee endow: In the Name of the Father, and of
the Son, and of the Holy Ghost. Amen."

This concludes the official ceremony and is followed
by the minister's blessing, prayers and a psalm.

As soon as it is over the minister will lead the way to
the vestry, followed in procession by the newly married
couple, the bridegroom's father with the bride's
mother, the bride's father with the bridegroom's

mother, the best man and the chief bridesmaid, the other bridesmaids and pages and perhaps one or two other important members of the couple's families if they are asked to do so.

In the vestry the bride signs the register – in her maiden name for the last time, followed by her husband, the minister and two witnesses. The witnesses should be selected in advance so that there is no confusion at the time – and usually comprise the best man and the chief bridesmaid.

As soon as the registration is completed, the organist will get the signal and immediately the bridal couple will start the recessional. The bride will march with her hand on her husband's left arm and with her veil thrown clear of her face.

The rest of the party will march behind in exactly the same order as they occupied on their way to the vestry. There is only one exception; the best man will have left the vestry alone and by the most convenient route to reach the church door in advance of the bridal party. As soon as the couple leave the porch, he will see them into their car.

There is likely to be considerable delay at this point. Amateur photography has captured the interests of many and a number of friends of the bride and bridegroom will take the opportunity, if the weather is fine, to photograph the newly weds, their bridesmaids, the official party – and indeed the church and the congregation, as it strolls out into the light of day.

As a sort of Master of Ceremonies, the best man needs to keep a check on the time. The whole party is due to arrive at the reception rooms at a pre-stated time - and if there is any unnecessary delay, the result may be a cold meal and a rush for trains afterwards.

The best man makes sure that the bride and her husband enter their car first – followed in succession by their parents, bridesmaids, family and guests.

The best man has still one duty to perform at the church before he leaves; he must settle the bridegroom's expenses in the form of marriage fees, organist's fees and any other out-of-pocket expenses that may have arisen on the spot.

Generally, he collects the marriage certificate too, and he may find it usual in that particular church, to make the various payments through the verger – with the exception, of course, of those belonging to the minister. However, if there is no opportunity to have a word with the clergyman afterwards, there is no objection to the fee being placed in a sealed envelope and given to the verger to be delivered in due course.

And if the guests are old-fashioned and untidy enough, the verger may be left with the task of clearing up the strewn confetti afterwards – and may justly expect some compensation for doing so.

The best man will need to perform these duties with the utmost speed. He will be expected at the photographer's studios, or wherever the official photographs are to be taken, almost as soon as the bridal party, and if he is wise, he will either have one of the ushers standing by with a car, or arrange for a taxi to be available.

A few additional reminders might be of value at this point.

(*a*) During the recessional there is no reason why the bridal couple should not smile and nod to their friends as they march down the nave – but there must be no pause or conversation inside the church. During the processional before the service, the attention of the bridal couple must not be allowed to wander. Their gaze should be directed towards the minister or the altar.

(*b*) Though it is usual for women to wear some form of headdress in church, there is no obligation on them to do so. This freedom applies only to the Church of England and in the case of some of the Free Churches. It does not apply in either a Roman Catholic Church or a Jewish synagogue.

(*c*) The strewing of confetti about church premises, either inside or outside, is frowned upon as untidy and creating unnecessary work for the verger.

(*d*) It has been known for the signing of the register to be delayed because of the lack of a pen and because, though a pen has been available, it contained no ink and that in the inkwell was no better than dried powder.

(*e*) If for some particular reason, a minister other

than the incumbent of the church where the wedding ceremony is to be held, is invited to conduct the service, it is usual to pay each of them the marriage fee. Such an invitation may be extended to a clergyman who happens to be a close relative or a particular friend of either the bride or the bridegroom.

(f) It is usually possible to have the church bells pealed for twenty minutes immediately prior to the ceremony and for up to half an hour afterwards. There will, of course, be an extra charge for this and the organist should be consulted together with the verger.

(g) If the wedding is to be an important public affair it might be well to have a rehearsal of the cere-mony on some day up to a week in advance of the actual event. Bridal gowns, suits and dresses are not needed for this purpose, though it is often wiser to provide some mock bouquets for the young brides-maids so that they may become accustomed to carrying them. Similarly, if a train is to be worn by the bride, a few yards of almost any material will suffice for the rehearsal.

Both the vicar and the verger should be consulted about the arrangements.

Though the ceremony is exactly the same where the bride happens to be a *widow*, tradition calls for less formality and suggests the omission of the bridal gown, orange blossom and the veil. Similarly the bridegroom should wear a dark lounge suit rather than the formal attire usual at a bride's "first" wedding.

Nor is the bride supported by bridesmaids, though a "dame of honour" usually attends her. The dame of honour may be chosen by her from amongst sisters of her own or the bridegroom's, or a close friend.

As there is no procession before the service, the dame of honour should wait for the bride at the chancel steps and her only duty is to relieve the bride of her bouquet.

Nor is there any obligation on anyone to "give the bride away", though she may invite her father or some other male relative to do so.

The pageantry of the ceremony is sadly missing, but the same restriction need not be placed on the reception afterwards – if there has been some lapse of time since the bride's first husband died.

In such case a wedding cake, floral decorations and speeches are quite permissible.

Other points include:

(*a*) The bridegroom should be attended by a best man. Ushers may be brought in, but as the ceremony is usually less ostentatious and less formal, there is rarely any need for them at a bride's "second" marriage.

(*b*) Not later than the day before her "second" wedding, the bride should remove her "first" wedding ring – and never wear it again.

(*c*) If the wedding takes place within a year of the first husband's death, the service and the reception afterwards should be confined to members of the bride and bridegroom's family and only a very few friends.

In such circumstances it is more appropriate, perhaps, to have the marriage performed in a registry office.

The marriage of a *widower* is much less restricted by convention than in the case of a widow. However, it is commonly less formal than a first wedding – but the decision is that of the bride. She should be humoured in the matter of the service, the formality, the number of guests and the scale of the reception afterwards.

The bride would be quite in order if she wore a bridal gown and a veil, was attended by bridesmaids and be "given away" by her father.

Though the Civil Law permits the re-marriage of *divorced persons*, it is forbidden by the law of the Church of England. Nor may a clergyman be compelled to permit the re-marriage of a divorced person, by anyone else, in his church.

This means that no marriage service can be performed in a church of the Church of England where either the bride or the bridegroom have a previous partner still living.

The marriage must therefore be a civil affair, generally speaking, conducted by a Registrar of Marriages in a Registry Office.

Such a marriage is a simple affair lasting but a few minutes. No religious service is involved and all that is required is that the marriage vows are exchanged and the register signed; two witnesses being present and signing as such.

No bridal gowns are worn and there is no pageantry. The bride may carry a bouquet offered by the bridegroom, but the office will have few, if any decorations and other than witnesses, there will be very few guests — if any.

However, the reception afterwards carries no restriction, though it is usual to confine the guests to those of first importance to the newly married pair.

Double Weddings; that is the marriage of two couples before the same minister or superintendent registrar of marriages, at the same time and in the same ceremony; are by no means rare occurrences. Less common, but still giving little cause for comment beyond the immediate neighbourhood, are ceremonies binding three separate couples in wedlock at the same time.

Larger groups are not unknown and indeed there is nothing to prohibit a mass wedding, linking together any number of couples at the same service.

However, the cause for such massive ceremonies is rare in this country and multiple weddings are more often than not, confined to family celebrations. Most common of all such occasions is the simultaneous marriage of sisters or of twins, to their chosen partners.

A double wedding calls for precisely the same detailed prior arrangements as those applicable to anybody about to marry. Each one of them must have the necessary qualifications, each of them must give the same notice; each couple must be separately licensed and, of course, distinct certificates of marriage will be issued to each of the couples.

The brides will have their own bridesmaids and a best man will be chosen by each of the bridegrooms. The brides will march down the aisle side-by-side to join their waiting bridegrooms. The two couples will then stand before the minister side-by-side, each bridegroom on the right of his bride.

The single ceremony will embrace both couples and only the responses will be made individually.

The recession must generally be made in separate parties because of the narrowness of the usual aisle, each party being complete in itself. The leading couple will assume that place by arrangement and not because of any "right", though it is usual to allow the elder of the two men to escort his bride and their attendants from the church first.

CHAPTER TWELVE

THE CEREMONY BY OTHER RITES AND CIVIL MARRIAGES

The Roman Catholic Church

There are two differing types of service for those marrying within the rites of the Roman Catholic Church. The more important is the "Solemn Wedding" where the service must be preceded by the reading of the banns on three successive Sundays, in the church of each of the bridal pair. The service is followed by Holy Mass, during which a special blessing is given to the bridal couple.

The Mass may be a "High Mass", requiring the participation of three priests and a choir, or a "Low Mass", either with or without music.

However, the Solemn Wedding is not permitted in the following instances:

(*a*) From the First Sunday of Advent until December 26th.

(*b*) From Ash Wednesday until Easter Monday.

(*c*) In the event of a "Mixed Marriage".

In all such cases a "Simple Wedding" must suffice and consists of no more than the blessing of the vows by a priest, in the presence of not fewer than two witnesses. The service is brief and lasts merely a matter of minutes – though it must be realized that the marriage is none the less binding in the eyes of the church.

A "Mixed Marriage" is that between a Roman Catholic and one baptized in some other faith – and the priest will require to see the baptismal certificate before undertaking to perform the ceremony.

A "Dispensation" is also required from the parish priest of the Catholic member of the bridal pair.

Three conditions are laid down for the granting of such a dispensation:

(a) the non-Catholic must undertake not to interfere with the religious belief and practices of the other.

(b) The wedding must take place in a Catholic Church and must not be preceded or followed by any other religious service.

(c) The children of the marriage must be brought up in the practice of the Catholic faith.

It is usual too, to expect the non-Catholic to receive a certain amount of religious instruction from the Catholic priest before the marriage, though this does not necessarily mean that he will be converted to the faith.

In the Simple Wedding the bride is conducted by her father to the bridegroom – and from there on he takes no further part in the ceremony and retires to his place in the front pew on the left of the nave.

The bride, on her bridegroom's left arm, leads the bridesmaids and the best man to the Sanctuary steps where the priest awaits them.

The chief bridesmaid stations herself on the bride's left after attending to the wedding veil and taking charge of the bridal bouquet and the bride's gloves. The best man stands to the right of the bridegroom – and the bridesmaids form into a line behind, facing the altar.

After the priest has proclaimed: "I join you together in marriage, in the Name of the Father and of the Son and of the Holy Ghost, Amen," he sprinkles them both with holy water.

The bridegroom then places the wedding ring, a piece of gold and a piece of silver on the prayer book in the priest's hand. The ring is blessed, after which the bridegroom presents the gold and silver to his bride and offers the ring, saying: "With this ring I thee wed; this gold and silver I give thee; with my body I thee worship; and with all my worldly goods I thee endow."

The bridegroom then places the ring on the thumb of the bride's left hand and says: "In the Name of the Father," transfers the ring to the bride's first finger and says, "And of the Son," – to the second finger, saying: "And of the Holy Ghost," and finally, as he slips the ring onto the bride's third finger, he concludes, "Amen."

Prayers follow to end the service proper.

In the case of a "Solemn Wedding", where Nuptial Mass follows as part of the ceremony, the bridal couple must fast for at least three hours before the Mass.

The bridal couple pass inside the Sanctuary rails –

the only occasion on which a Catholic woman is permitted to be within the Sanctuary – while the bridesmaids and the best man retire in procession to the pews; the chief bridesmaid to the front pew on the left of the nave and best man on the right. The bridesmaids sit behind, two to each pew – and room should of course, be left for them.

If Holy Communion is to be received by the bridesmaids and the parents of the bride and bridegroom, they will join the newly married pair at the communicants' rail.

When the Mass is concluded and the bride and bridegroom leave the Sanctuary, the bridesmaids and the best man take their places again; the chief bridesmaid on the right arm of the best man; behind the bridal couple and with the bridesmaids in pairs to follow – and move in the recessional down the aisle to the church door. From there to their cars – and the whole party proceed to the scene of the wedding reception.

There is one interruption to the religious service in the church. As the service is not legally binding in itself, in English law, a civil declaration has to be made at some stage. Custom has it that this follows after the religious service is concluded, in the case of "Mixed Marriages", and immediately prior to Nuptial Mass in the event of a "Solemn Wedding."

At this point the bridal couple, together with not fewer than two witnesses proceed to the Sacristy to make their declaration and to sign the register.

A few points to be remembered include:

(*a*) The bride signs the register in her maiden name – for the last time.

(*b*) The witnesses who are to sign the register should be chosen in advance to avoid confusion. The best man and the chief bridesmaid are often selected, but each should be 21 years of age or over.

(*c*) The remarriage of divorced persons is strictly refused in the Catholic Church. However, there may be cases where the previous marriage is not recognized by the church, perhaps because it did not comply with church law as in the case of those who were first married in a civil registry office.

(*d*) In any event, in view of the complicated requirements of the Catholic clergy, in their different degrees, it is essential to consult the priest who is to conduct the service, well in advance: in the case of a "Mixed Marriage", months beforehand.

The Free Churches

In the majority of Free Church denominations the church itself will have been registered by a Superintendent Registrar of Marriages as a building in which marriages may be solemnized. Ministers of the Baptist, Congregational, Methodist, Presbyterian and other divisions of the Protestant faith, have long taken advantage of their rights, under the Marriage Act of 1898, to become registered by a Registrar of Marriages as "authorized" persons; that is, to have applied for and received sanction both to conduct the service and to act as the registrar under the civil law.

Others, for various reasons, have not sought such authority and in consequence, though they may conduct a marriage ceremony, a Registrar of Marriages must be present to record the wedding, or a separate, civil ceremony must be conducted by a Registrar of Marriages in his office.

Wherever the venue of a marriage, the register must be signed by the bridal couple after they have made their vows and the fact must be witnessed by the signature of two onlookers.

In all cases, the order of service is a matter left almost entirely to the religious scruples of the couple who are to be married, and of course, to the special rites of the church whose blessing they seek.

Certain requirements must be met in the solemnization of all Free Church weddings. They are:

(*a*) Both the bride and the bridegroom must be at least 21 years of age or have the written consent of their parents.

(*b*) They must be unmarried or legally divorced.

(*c*) Proper notice must have been given of the intention to marry in accordance with the civil law.

(*d*) The service must take place in a registered building.

(*e*) The minister must be an authorized person, or a Registrar of Marriages must be present, or a separate service must be conducted in the Registrar's office.

(*f*) At some point in the service the following declarations must be made in the presence of the minister, if he is an authorized person – or before a Registrar:

> (i) "I do solemnly declare that I know not of any lawful impediment why I.......... may not be joined in matrimony to.........."
>
> (ii) To each other in turn, "I call upon these persons here present to witness that I .... do take thee,.......... to my lawful wedded husband (or wife, as the case may be)."

(*g*) Each must sign the marriage register as should two witnesses of the marriage in proof thereof.

The variety of detail in the ceremonies of the different sects is considerable – sometimes merely a matter of detail, often they are fundamental.

In almost every case, however, the order of service follows, roughly, that customary in the Church of England, some of the details of which include:

1. The procession.

2. The bride stands before the minister to the left of her bridegroom, during the service. Her father, or whoever is to give her away, on her left. The best man stands on the right of the bridegroom.

3. The service begins with the betrothal.

4. The minister will call upon the congregation to voice any legal objection to the marriage.

5. The wedding ring is blessed and the couple exchange vows – as required by law.

6. Receive the blessing of the church.

7. Sign the register.

In all cases the minister concerned should be consulted well in advance of the projected date of the wedding. Some churches are more pretentious in their ceremonial than others, some more formal and yet others, almost entirely devoid of pageantry.

Although it is general for the Free Churches to view a marriage as binding for life, it is usually within the discretion of each minister to regard the remarriage of a divorced person as he might think fit in the particular case put before him.

Some ministers may be found to be adamant in their refusal to marry a person who has been divorced, others will take cognizance of who was the injured party and yet others may consider the whole circumstances – even to the point of charity. Obviously the most careful enquiries need to be made by the couple concerned, before completing any arrangements, in such an event.

The Quakers

A Quaker marriage is very different to most other wedding services. It is extremely simple and altogether free of ceremonial.

The first step to such a marriage needs to be taken at least six weeks in advance of the proposed date, when the couple apply to the Registering Officer of the Liberating Monthly Meeting for a copy of Marriage Form A. This needs to be completed by both the bride and the bridegroom.

The form requires and contains:

(*a*) A joint declaration of the intention to marry, intimating the proposed time and date for the event.

(*b*) An application by either of the parties, who may not be a member of the Society of Friends, to be married in accordance with their practices. Such an application must be supported by not less than two recommendations from members of the Society of Friends.

(*c*) Where one or both parties is not in membership of the Society, the Registering Officer needs to issue a certificate of permission. If the couple live in different districts or worship at different Meeting Houses, a certificate is required from each of the Registering Officers. The refusal of one is sufficient to ban the service.

(*d*) The couple must then make application to marry in accordance with civil law through the Superintendent Registrar of Marriages in the district in which they live – or if they live in different districts, notice must be given to the Registrar in each.

(*e*) At the same time, notice of the intended marriage

is given by the Quaker Registering Officer at the first Sunday morning Meeting where the couple usually worship, or within the district in which they live.

(*f*) 7 days later, if there has been no objection to the marriage, the Registering Officer will complete a form certifying the fact.

(*g*) When certificates have been issued both by the Registering Officer of the Liberating Monthly Meeting and the Superintendent Registrar of Marriages, the Monthly Meeting in the district where the marriage is to take place, will decide on a suitable time and date for the event.

The service takes the Quaker form of silent, personal worship. There is neither pageantry nor music, set service nor sermon. Only those who may feel the spirit move them will either rise to speak, or kneel to pray.

There is rarely a bridesmaid or a best man, a bridal gown and a morning coat are unusual; there is neither a procession nor a recessional afterwards.

But at some point during the meeting the bride and bridegroom will rise and hand-in-hand make their declaration of marriage.

The bridegroom will say:

> "Friends, I take this my friend . . . . to be my wife, promising, through Divine assistance, to be unto her a loving and faithful husband so long as we both on earth shall live."

The bride makes a similar statement. The wedding

certificate is then signed by the bridal couple and by two of the witnesses. The certificate is then read aloud by the Registering Officer and after the meeting, it is usual for all others present to add their names to the certificate.

The wedding ring plays no part in the marriage, though it is usual for the couple either to exchange rings afterwards, or for the bridegroom to give one to his bride.

The remarriage of a divorced person, though frowned upon by the Society of Friends, does not meet with a flat refusal. Despite the solemnity of the first occasion, the Quakers view a subsequent divorce as perhaps an inevitable separation of the spirit of two anti-pathetic souls – irreconcilable and complete. In such an event the Monthly Meeting might well appoint a committee of Friends in whom they have confidence, to consider the matter in all its details and to make a decision without the need for undue discussion by the full Meeting.

The Jewish Wedding

The first requirement of a Jewish wedding is the compliance with the civil law and the civil ceremony usually takes place in the office of the Registrar of Marriages in the district where the religious service is to be held – some hours in advance.

A Jewish wedding may only take place between two Jews, and before the religious ceremony, the couple will be asked by the Jewish Secretary for Marriages for evidence that their parents were married in accordance with Jewish rites.

The actual ceremony may take place anywhere – be it in the home of one of the couple, in a hall where a reception is to be held afterwards or, as is general today, in a synagogue. It may take place on any day, at any time, with the exception of the Sabbath – from sunset on a Friday to sunset on a Saturday. Certain days of festival are also barred.

Wherever the ceremony is held, it is necessary to have a quorum of not fewer than ten people present to witness the event.

It is customary for the bridal couple to attend divine service on the Sabbath preceding the wedding, accompanied by the father of each of them. During the service the bridegroom and close relatives will be honoured by being called upon to read passages from the Scroll of the Law.

On the wedding day, the bride and bridegroom are expected to fast and to offer up private prayers for the forgiveness of past sins so that they may enter upon their new life strengthened by divine grace.

The bride wears a veil for her wedding, long sleeves and gloves. The bridegroom and the male members of the party usually wear morning coats, striped trousers and grey wedding ties. Everybody present, including the male members of the party, must have their heads covered.

The bridegroom arrives at the synagogue first, accompanied by his father, the bride's father and other male members of the two families.

As soon as the bride arrives, the bridegroom is conducted by his escort to his place under the canopy. The escort then returns to the door to escort the bride into the synagogue.

The procession then consists of the bride on her father's right arm, the bridesmaids, the bridegroom's parents and her own mother. After them comes other relatives of both.

In this fashion, the bride is brought under the canopy to stand on the right of her bridegroom. The bridesmaids and other ladies in the procession take their places behind the bride, while the best man and the male members of the official party stand behind the bridegroom – all facing the minister and the Ark.

A blessing of welcome is pronounced by the minister and this blessing may be accompanied by a choir. A psalm is chanted – usually the Psalm of Thanksgiving, (Psalm 100), followed by an address to the couple by the minister.

Then comes the Betrothal Blessing after which the bridegroom places the wedding ring on the second finger of the bride's right hand and makes the following declaration:

"Behold, thou art consecrated unto me by this ring according to the law of Moses and of Israel."

This declaration consummates the marriage in most orthodox synagogues, but in more Liberal, or Reform communities, there are some varieties in the service.

The orthodox service is followed by the reading of the Marriage Contract in both Aramaic and in English.

The seven bendictions are then chanted by the minister:

1. The Blessing over the cup of wine.

2. The Praise of God as creator of the universe.

3. As Creator of man.

4. As Creator of woman.

5. Prayer for the comfort of Zion.

6. Prayer for the rejoicing of the young couple.

7. Prayer for their joint happiness and for the restoration of joy and gladness in the cities of Judah and in the streets of Jerusalem.

A wine glass is then set on the floor before the bridegroom who breaks it under his heel – to remind the couple, in the midst of their joy, that sad events also exist in life, such as the breaking up and destruction of the Temple in Jersalem of old, and that against all such breaches in life, their home, symbolized by the canopy over their heads, must be conducted so as to earn divine protection.

The ceremony ends with the pronouncement by the minister, of the ancient, priestly benediction:–

"The Lord bless you and keep you, the Lord make His face to shine upon you and be gracious unto you, the Lord lift up His countenance upon you and give you peace."

If the couple have not already been married in a Register Office, they must now sign the register, together with the marriage register of the synagogue, which must also bear the signatures of two witnesses and of the Jewish Secretary for Marriages.

Civil Marriages

Often, for various reasons, a couple may prefer to marry free of any religious obligations. It may be that they have different, irreconcilable, religious beliefs; maybe divorce has cut one or both of them off from their church, or possibly, family objections have decided them to marry privately and without more than the minimum of ceremony necessary to make public and legal, their new status.

Under a certificate of marriage obtainable from a Superintendent Registrar of Marriages, anyone legally entitled to marry, must be married by him not less than twenty-one days after due notice has been given and published. Where the couple apply for a licence and satisfy the legal requirements for the issue of such a document – as detailed in Chapter 4, the ceremony may be performed by the Registrar after the expiration of one clear day.

Such a marriage entails no religious service; all that is expected is that the following vows will be exchanged before a Registrar and two witnesses:

> "I do solemnly declare that I know not of any legal impediment why I ...... may not be joined in matrimony to ...... "
> and to one another in turn: "I call upon these persons here present to witness that I ...... do take thee, ... to my lawful wedded husband (or "wife", as the case may be)."

Then follows the signing of the marriage register by each of the newlyweds and those witnessing the event.

The symbol of the wedding ring from the bridegroom to the bride is common practice, but has no legal significance under civil law.

A Superintendent Registrar of Marriages has no legal right to refuse to remarry a divorced person. The civil law takes no cognizance of religious beliefs or scruples in such cases and so long as the decree absolute has been granted and all other legal requirements have been met, the Registrar is duty bound to perform the marriage ceremony.

CHAPTER THIRTEEN

CELEBRATIONS

THERE are two most suitable places in which to hold the wedding reception after the church service. One is, of course, in the home of the bride's parents and the second, and more usual today, is in a hotel, restaurant or similar establishment.

The modern house is generally too small in which to entertain more than a limited number of guests and rarely big enough to accommodate all those who expect and feel entitled, to be invited.

Probably too, the bride's mother is unwilling to be burdened with the chores of cooking and acting as waitress and dishwasher on the side, to a cheerful but hungry crowd of guests, while her husband doubles as barman and cloakroom attendant.

The bride's parents will be required, in due course, to be photographed with the bridal couple – free of a kitchenmaid's apron and a barman's shirt-sleeves. The bride's father will probably be called upon to propose the toast of "The Health and Happiness of the Bride and Bridegroom", while the bride's mother answers the door to a succession of telegraph boys and stray guests, and sees to her daughter's change into a "going-away" outfit after the meal.

And both of them, as host and hostess, must receive their guests on arrival, entertain them during the reception and see them on their way home afterwards!

Yet, despite the tribulations of a reception held at home, some brave, competent mothers still prefer to face the drudgery of such a service, looking upon it as some sort of last, probably misunderstood gesture, to a departing daughter – and who shall deny them the right?

If indeed the bride's home is to be used for the reception, her mother will need to plan the venture well in advance. What room – and rooms – has she available?

A hall, the larger the better of course, is needed as a reception room where the host, hostess, the bridegroom's parents and the bride and bridegroom can receive and welcome their guests.

Unless the hall is very large, the need to keep the guests moving is paramount – unless the room is to be choked and the queue of visitors brought to a standstill.

The bride's brothers and sisters, the bridesmaids and, if necessary, the best man, should be briefed to keep the flow of guests passing beyond the reception point towards the main rooms and the cloakrooms, without pause.

As they arrive, the guests should shake hands with the bride's mother first and then her father. Immediately afterwards they meet the bridegroom's parents followed by the bride and bridegroom, in that order.

And to prevent a hold-up, the newlyweds' parents and afterwards, the newlyweds themselves, should make their greetings brief and save any protracted conversation until all the guests have been received.

If the house is large enough a room should be set aside for the display of wedding presents, but where this is not practicable, they can be exhibited in the same room where the buffet has been set out or round the walls of the dining-room.

As soon as they have been received, the guests should take the opportunity to inspect the presents and over this they will find the chance to converse more freely – and for the two families to get to know one another better.

When the time comes for the meal, the bride and bridegroom should lead the way into the dining-room and to their places at the top of the table. They should be followed by the bride's father in company with the bridegroom's mother and the bride's mother on the arm of the bridegroom's father.

As, almost certainly, the bride's mother will be busy in the kitchen and her father still pouring drinks behind the mock-up bar, it is probable that the bridegroom's parents will follow the newlyweds. After them comes the chief bridesmaid on the arm of the best man, the bridesmaids – and the rest of the guests.

Where a luncheon or other meal is to be served, the bride and bridegroom sit at the head of the table; the bride on her husband's left. The bride's mother sits next to the bridegroom and the bridegroom's mother on the left of the bride's father who sits next to his newly married daughter.

Groom's Father	Bride's Mother	Groom	Bride	Bride's Father	Groom's Mother

The Cake

In the centre of the table immediately in front of the newlyweds, stands the cake.

Where the meal is a buffet sideboard or table, the bride and bridegroom usually stand to one side of it, probably behind a small table bearing the wedding cake. Refreshments are then handed round, either by staff engaged for the purpose, or more frequently, by the bridesmaids, the ushers and members of the bride's family.

So that the guests may move about freely during the meal, most of the furniture should be cleared from the room in advance, but it must be remembered that Granny is probably present and may find the long spell on her feet too much. Chairs must therefore be made available for guests of her age – probably set around the walls to conserve space.

Suggestions for the table are contained in Chapter 15 as are a few recommended wines.

As soon as the guests appear to have reached the end of their meal, the toasts are drunk. The best man acts as toastmaster and it is he who calls on the first speaker when he thinks the time is ripe. This is either a close personal friend or relative of the bride – often, her father. The toast is: "The Health and Happiness of the Bride and Bridegroom".

The speech is usually of a semi-serious nature, especially if it is made by the father and generally includes :–

1. The happiness he and his wife have experienced in the bringing up of their daughter, the treasure she has been to them and the sad miss that must inevitably follow her marriage and move to a home of her own.

2. A couple of interludes in her life – one, perhaps amusing, the other more serious.

3. A welcome into the family, of the new son-in-law and the offer of a place at their table for the future.

4. A welcome too, to the bridegroom's parents.

5. Perhaps an episode concerning the bride and the bridegroom together – particularly if they have known one another for a number of years.

6. A little timely advice to the newly-weds, usually bound up with his own experiences in company with his wife – the bride's mother.

7. The toast of the Health and Happiness of the couple.

Of course this is merely a suggestion and it is probable that the proposer will have other things to say and other points to make. But he must make his speech with one eye on the clock – and the faces of his guests. The bride probably has a train to catch – and the guests are easily bored by a lengthy monologue.

The bridegroom responds to the toast – and in his turn proposes a toast to the "Bridesmaids".

The first part of his speech should be serious and directed particularly towards his own parents. The second part must be devoted to the bridesmaids and be given a much less serious turn.

In the first part, responding to the toast proposed by the bride's father, or whoever has made it, the bridegroom might refer to:

1. The kindness of his parents during his boyhood, their care and attention to his upbringing.

2. The thanks he owes them for his start in life – and of any particular present they have given him of that nature.

3. A tribute to his wife's parents – and anything they may have provided for their future.

4. Perhaps a short episode of his meeting with his bride, of their engagement, difficulties or fortunes.

5. His intention to devote himself to the happiness of his bride.

And at this point the bridegroom may turn his attention to lighter matters and his toast to the bridesmaids, with perhaps:

6. Thanks to his best man for his assistance and possible nuisance value.

7. A reference to the beauty of the bridesmaids and his thanks for their help during the service.

At this point, if he has provided some small present for each of the young ladies, he will call them forward one after another to receive his gift.

Such presents are by no means mandatory and where given they usually comprise some small piece of artificial jewellery.

The best man replies to the toast on behalf of the bridesmaids. It is usually made in a completely amusing vein and is designed to take the last of the seriousness out of the celebration. He might refer to:

1. The bridegroom's luck in getting the bride he has – and how many another man has wept over her poor choice.

2. The difficulty in getting a scared bridegroom to the altar.

3. The joy he and his friends feel at getting rid of him from their bachelor ranks and their pity for an unfortunate bride.

4. And, of course, the thanks of the bridesmaids for the presents and good wishes they have received from the bridegroom.

This ends the official speeches – those ordained by custom. Others may follow, but they should be kept short, amusing and with an eye to how much is left in the glasses and bottles with which to drink the toasts.

Next, the best man opens and reads the telegrams that have been received. Most of them will be addressed to the couple but where any are addressed to the man, they should contain congratulations; to the girl, wishes for her happiness. A bride should not be congratulated on her marriage!

As they are delivered, the telegrams should be placed unopened in front of the best man for this item on the programme. He should read them with what humour he can find – bearing in mind that a long list of similar telegrams can become boring. After the reception, the best man should hand the telegrams to the bride's mother to be kept for her until after her honeymoon. It is the bride's duty to acknowledge them all when she returns – though this can often be conveniently combined with the letters of thanks for the presents received.

Then comes the cutting of the wedding cake.

The bride cuts through the cake with her husband's hand covering hers in a gesture of help. They may cut a complete slice and share it between them, but due to the elaborate decorations on many cakes, the inexperience of the couple and the probable nervousness of the bride, they rarely make more than a token cut. After that the cake is cut into portions by the bride's mother and the slices are handed round to the guests by the bridesmaids.

Everyone is expected at least to sample the cake – and much of it is kept to be dispatched in small portions, in tiny boxes to friends and relatives who have been unable to attend the reception – perhaps because of age, distance or illness.

The bride then retires to change into her "going-away" outfit and as soon as she returns, all ready to leave for her honeymoon, the farewells should be said as briefly as possible. She and her husband may have a train to catch or a schedule to keep – and besides, there will have been a sufficient display of the emotions by now. More could mean embarrassment to all concerned.

The parents should be the last to make their farewells – and not until then should any of the guests depart.

The inadequacy of the modern home, the tremendous amount of work involved and the heartbreaking clearing-up afterwards usually persuades the bride's parents to hold the reception in more convenient circumstances, under the supervision of an expert caterer in rooms, or an establishment designed for the purpose.

Most medium and large hotels have the facilities and often specialize in the organization of such functions. Their staff will cook and serve almost any meal desired, they will provide the wines and give expert advice on the subject, they will arrange the tables, the the decorations, the cloakrooms, the reception room, the dining-room, a room for the display of the newly-wed's presents – and even set aside a place where the bridal photographs can be taken.

However, arrangements for the reception in this manner need to be made well in advance – weeks, as a rule.

Nor does the organization of the function by a caterer altogether excuse the host and hostess from making any of the arrangements. The hotelier will not, or cannot decide the following points:

(a) The menu.

(b) The wines.

(c) Who is to provide the cake – and to choose it?

(d) What flowers are to be used on the tables – and who provides them?

(e) The number of guests to be present.

(f) The seating plan.

(g) The bride's changing room.

(h) and of course, the time and the date.

The first thing to understand is that the reception after the service is intended to allow the wedding guests to congratulate and felicitate the newlyweds, to witness the cutting of the cake in ceremonial fashion, to join in the toasts to the health and happiness of the couple – and to give the families of each of them an opportunity to mix and get to know one another better.

The meal itself is incidental to the celebrations and is

served because the guests will be hungry long before the bride and the bridegroom depart for their honeymoon – particularly if they have travelled far for the service earlier in the day. And as the meal has always been an essential need, it has long been the custom to use it for the high-spot features of the celebrations. During it, the toasts are given, the cake cut and the telegrams read to the guests.

In consequence, the menu, the wines and the seating arrangements warrant a great deal of thought and careful planning – indeed, the whole function, from the reception to the departure of the newlyweds, requires meticulous organization.

There are many methods and fashions in which to conduct a ceremonial wedding breakfast – or luncheon, as is more usual; or even an afternoon tea. Few of the arrangements are obligatory, though custom lays down certain broad high-lights; the order of precedence is of little importance, provided that everybody understands that it is the day of the "newlyweds" – and the menu and wines may be chosen freely by the host and hostess, so long as they remember that liquid refreshment will be needed when the toasts are proposed.

Under the circumstances, the method and organization described here are those generally adopted by the author and may be freely adapted to suit the needs of the occasion and the pleasure of those who are to attend.

ADVANCE ARRANGEMENTS

The wedding cake. The cake must be ordered some weeks in advance of the wedding and apart from the style and decorations, its size should be considered in relation both to the number of guests who are expected to attend the reception and to those, who though unable to be present, will expect to receive a portion by mail.

The cake should be delivered by the confectioner to the caterer at the venue of the reception on the night before the wedding. Though, of course, there is no absolute need for him to have it until an hour or so before the guests are due at the reception rooms, its early arrival will save a lot of worry and the possibility of a last minute disappointment.

The flowers. The caterer will be glad to receive the flowers that have been ordered by the bride's mother for the tables and display stands, as early as possible on the morning of the reception. He has a great deal of preparatory work to do before the guests arrive, not least of it concerned with the decorations.

Besides the flowers for the table, blooms will be required for the display stands in the reception room, the dining-room and in the room set aside for the exhibition of the wedding presents.

A posy is probably needed too, for the top of the wedding cake.

Menus and other printed material. Details of the menu

and wines will have been settled between the hosts and the caterer some weeks in advance of the wedding date – and these should have been sent to a printer immediately afterwards. At the same time the hosts will have had the opportunity to have paper serviettes printed, bearing the names of the newlyweds – and the printer will have offered to provide the place-cards on which the names of the guests should be written to mark their places at table.

All these should be in the hands of the caterer not later than the day before the wedding – not forgetting the need to complete the writing up of the place-cards!

The reception rooms. Although the rooms required for the reception will have been agreed with the caterer some time in advance, there are still a few arrangements in this connection that must be completed by the hosts. These are chiefly concerned with the exhibition of the wedding presents.

As they are likely to be laid out on trestle tables, tiered on boxes and covered overall with white tablecloths, the caterer will want to know in good time exactly what he must provide in the way of furniture. Nothing looks worse than a stacked heap of surplus tables and chairs that could well have been taken out of the room, if time had been allowed for the purpose.

This information should be supplied to the caterer at least 24 hours before the event – naturally, the hosts themselves will not know the answer to that problem until the presents have been received.

On the afternoon before the wedding, the hosts, the bride and bridegroom and the best man, should take the parcels and cases to the room laid aside for the purpose – and make their own display of the presents, together with the necessary name-cards, floral decorations and not forgetting to remove the wrappings and boxes afterwards. The caterer will see to the clearing up of straw, paper and other rubbish.

If the presents are valuable, they should be insured to include their display. Though the caterer will do his very best to safeguard them overnight and during the reception, he is unlikely to accept responsibility for theft or damage. He will most certainly lock up the exhibition room immediately after the presents have been set out and those responsible for its arrangements have left, but he is unlikely to part with the key. He must have access in case of fire or other hazards.

The caterer will unlock the room when the guests are due to arrive – but it is up to the bridal party to remove the presents afterwards.

The seating arrangements. The caterer will need to have some idea of how many guests are to be entertained some time in advance of the event – and he should be given final details, together with the seating plan and the place-cards not later than the evening before the wedding.

There are certain formalities concerning the seating arrangements – though a hostess should not distress herself if she finds it more convenient, or a happier solution, to seat people in some other manner.

This plan cannot be made without the assistance of the caterer who will advise on the layout of the tables to suit the numbers involved, the shape and style of the dining-room and the service points.

The top table is the most important and the main pre-occupation of the planner and the simplest arrangement is that already give on page 143.

For an extension to that plan, the following is generally a happy arrangement: *(See opposite)*

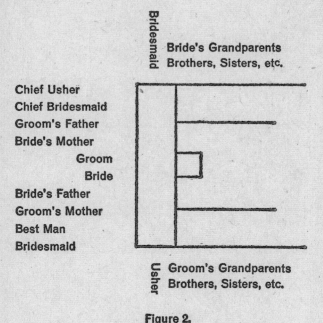

Figure 2.

The brothers and sisters should be interspersed by their wives and husbands – where applicable. Uncles and aunts follow and then the friends of the newlyweds.

Though the above is the author's preferred seating arrangement, others insist that there should be a host occupying the middle seat on the top table. He is usually the bride's father and on his right sits the bride and her groom.

Such a plan might look like this:

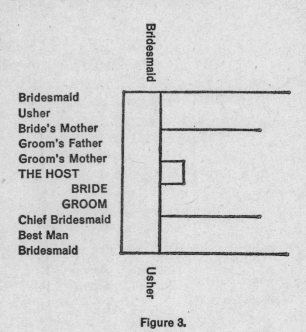

Figure 3.

The length of the side tables will depend largely on the size and shape of the room and the number of guests to be seated.

Where possible only the outer sides should be used so that everybody has a clear view of everybody else.

Usually this is impracticable – or the tables are

made to stretch out at such a length that those towards the foot of each arm will be out of touch with the top table. In such case the inner sides of the two arms should be used.

In no circumstances should the inner side of the top table be used for seating purposes. The cake, on a small, separate table in front of the bridal couple, should be the only thing to screen their faces.

Of course even larger layouts may be used:

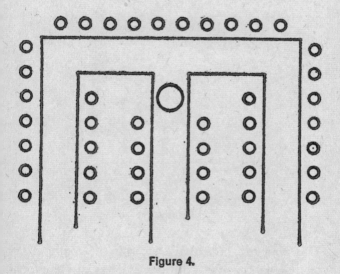

Figure 4.

And for numbers in excess of, perhaps, 200, an

attractive arrangement can be made in the following manner, where not one of the guests will have their back fully turned towards the newlyweds:

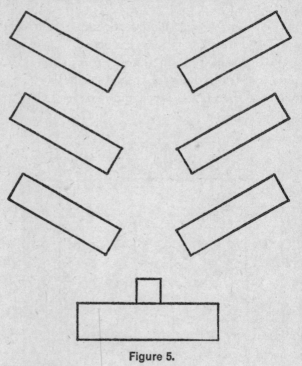

Figure 5.

This plan can be extended to suit the room, either by adding extra sprigs if the room is long, or by lengthening those shown if it is broad.

However, your caterer will have expert knowledge of the facilities of his own dining-room or banqueting hall and his advice must be sought.

After due consideration has been given to the arrangement for seating the members of the two families, their husbands and wives, and the friends of the bride and bridegroom, an attempt should be made to alternate the sexes as far as possible. And a good hostess will give thought to the problem of family feuds, jealousies and friendships.

Such likes and dislikes, if they are not sorted out before the reception, may well lead to quarrels, unhappy silences and outspoken comments. To separate anti-pathetic guests irrespective of their seating "rights", is much better than to leave matters to take their course and hope for the best. This is the newlyweds "day" and every effort must be made to keep it free of friction.

"Off-beat" guests might well be kept at a distance from the top table, humourists kept apart and younger couples with a personal interest in one another, placed happily side-by-side.

The suggestion is that the bride's family and friends should occupy the tables on the bridegroom's side of the room – and vice versa, but others will persuade the host and hostess that the families should be mixed as freely as possible. Both arrangements have a lot to commend them to the hostess. Mixing the families does tend to give them an opportunity to get to know one another, while segregation means less embarrass-ment to all concerned.

The table plan, with each seat containing the name of a guest, should be given to the caterer to post up in a convenient place so that the guests will be able to go straight to their places as they enter the dining-room – and confirm the actual seat by means of the place-card bearing his or her name, lying on the table by the plate.

All ready? The table will be set and probably, if the first course is cold, it will be pre-served.

The wines, if they are white, should be chilling in ice buckets or standing in cooling shelves; if it is red, the bottles should be in the dining-room for an hour or more before the meal to adjust themselves to room temperature.

The photographer should be ready with his equipment in the room set aside for the purpose.

The commissionaire, or doorman, should be outside on the pavement ready to open the car doors – and to keep a space free of parked vehicles immediately opposite the entrance.

The hall porter must be ready to direct the guests to the apartments allocated for the function and the cloakroom attendants ready to receive the cloaks, coats and wraps.

Port, sherry and cordials should be poured into glasses ready to be served as the guests arrive and the waitresses briefed to move among them with their trays all prepared and loaded with the reception drinks.

THE ARRIVAL

Though the newlyweds leave the church first, it is important that the bride's parents arrive first at the reception rooms. As host and hostess they must be the first to greet their guests as they arrive.

The reception line should consist of:

The Bride's Mother
The Bride's Father
The Bridegroom's Mother
The Bridegroom's Father
The Bride
The Bridegroom

in that order.

If the reception is to include a buffet meal, the reception by both sets of parents and the newlyweds, almost invariably takes place immediately on the arrival of the guests at the reception rooms, but if there is to be a luncheon, it is quite usual for the actual reception of the guests to take place later, as they pass into the dining-room.

This is often preferred as it relieves the parents and the newlyweds of the duty to rush to the reception rooms from the church; giving the bride time to recover her composure, for the photographer to take his pictures without the need for the guests to have to kick their heels as they wait and for the guests to get rid of their cloaks and prepare themselves to meet the receptionists.

We will assume that the reception is to take place immediately on the arrival of the guests, for the moment.

Guests are greeted by their hosts and the bridal couple as they arrive – without regard to family seniority. The greetings must be brief if there is not to be a long line of impatiently waiting guests and the best man and bridesmaids should do their best to move them on by directing them towards the already poured drinks.

They should be encouraged too, to circulate about the room, to meet one another – and of course, take the opportunity to inspect the wedding presents.

The guests should arrive as promptly as maybe so that the bridal party can finish with the greetings as soon as possible and retire to the venue set apart for the taking of photographs.

THE PHOTOGRAPHS

In fine, summery weather the photographer may have taken the opportunity to get most of his pictures in the setting provided by the church precincts, but too often the weather is unsuitable or the season unwelcoming.

Generally the caterer will have arranged a suitable room for the purpose though often enough, as some shots will be required of the bride and bridegroom cutting the cake, the dining-room is used.

The photographs usually consist of at least one of the bride and bridegroom; the couple with the best man, bridesmaids and ushers; the couple with their parents – and grandparents, and of the whole bridal party.

Other photographs may be called for at the bidding of those present – often of the bride alone and with her bridesmaids.

The photograph of the "cutting" of the wedding cake is usually a pretence; the bride holding the knife in place and her husband's hand covering hers – but saving the actual ceremony until later in the proceedings.

THE WEDDING MEAL

As soon as the photographs have been taken, the best man should lead the couple and other members of the bridal party to where their guests are conversing and drinking their apéritifs. They may join them for a while but must avoid standing in cliques or of allowing anyone to monopolize their attention.

They may spend a few minutes inspecting their wedding presents and discussing them with their guests – but the best man must keep his eye on the time.

As soon as the caterer or one of his staff indicates that the meal is ready, he should persuade the newlyweds to move towards the dining-room arm-in-arm.

Often the caterer will lead them to their places at the top table, sometimes to music but more often in easy, welcoming conversation.

Behind the newlyweds, the bridal party should enter

the dining-room in the following order:

    The bride's father with the bridegroom's mother,
    The bridegroom's father with the bride's mother,
    The best man with the chief bridesmaid,
    The bridesmaids,
    The pages – and,
    The guests.

Before entering the dining-room the guests should have examined the seating plan and so, with the help of the place-cards, should have little difficulty in locating their seats.

When everybody has found his or her place, the minister who has conducted the wedding ceremony will say grace – that is, if he has been invited and is present. If he is not at the reception any other clergyman among the guests may say it – though more often than not the duty falls onto the shoulders of the bride's father.

Grace is often neglected nowadys – but should never be omitted if a minister of religion is present.

Suggestions for menus and the accompanying wines are made in Chapter 15.

THE SPEECHES

When the coffee stage is reached, the best man should call for order and prompt the bride's father to rise to propose the toast of "The health and happiness of the bride and bridegroom."

Though it is usual for this toast to be given by the

bride's father – or guardian – it is not uncommon for that duty to be passed to some other male member of the bride's family who is deemed to be perhaps a better speaker or is someone of note. But the bride's father must remember to delegate such a task some days in advance and not have it sprung on some unsuspecting guest at the last moment.

A few suggestions for the content of this speech have been made earlier in this chapter and need not be repeated.

The bridegroom then replies on behalf of his wife and himself, thanking the gathering for their good wishes, their parents for being their parents and all those who have helped to make the wedding ceremony and the reception a success – concluding with the bridesmaids, and in so doing proposes a toast to "The bridesmaids".

The best man invariably responds on behalf of the young ladies. His speech should be light and as far as possible filled with humour. From this point there should be no return to emotional references or serious topics – and the ability to make such a speech is often taken very much into consideration by the bridegroom when choosing his best man.

Those three speeches compose the traditional toasts and replies customary in a wedding reception. No further speeches need be given and as often as not, they are considered sufficient – but it is by no means uncommon, where time permits, for other guests to speak. One most frequently favoured is a speech of thanks to the host and hostess, given usually by some relative of the bridegroom's – followed by a reply from the bride's father, very briefly if he has already spoken.

Other speeches are permissible, though the greatest need is to avoid boredom – particularly by insincere guests who like the sound of their own voices or who cannot bear not to have taken some noteworthy part in the proceedings.

With one eye on the time, the best man brings the speeches to an end by rising to open and read the telegrams of congratulations and good wishes that have arrived for the newlyweds. In reading them he should endeavour to introduce a few light, background comments on the contents and about those who have sent them. The reading of a large number of telegrams can soon become boring; they are usually repetitious and many of the names will be known to few of the guests.

The bridegroom should remember to hand the telegrams to the bride either immediately after the reception or more usually, on her return from her honeymoon. It is her duty to write and acknowledge them as soon as possible afterwards – generally at the same time as she writes her thanks to those who have sent presents.

THE CAKE

The ceremony of cutting the cake follows. The caterer or one of his staff will assist the bride to place the point of the knife in the correct place near the centre of the bottom tier of the cake and with the cutting edge towards her.

The bridegroom places a hand over his wife's and slowly and carefully helps her to force the point of the blade down into the heart of the cake and then to draw the blade forward and downwards.

Usually that completes the formal "Cutting" of the cake. The gesture is merely a token operation designed to prevent unnecessary damage to the cake and its sugary decorations. The caterer takes over from that point and after dismantling the tiers and ornaments, uses his expertise to divide up a portion of the cake into handy, not overlarge slices. He plates the segments and the bridesmaids distribute them amongst the guests. If there is a large number of guests, the catering staff will help the distribution.

The remainder of the cake will then be set aside for eventual distribution to friends and relatives of the newlyweds who have been unable to attend the wedding and the reception afterwards.

It is traditional for the bridesmaids to keep their slices of cake and to place them under their pillows that night – in the belief that they will then dream of their own future husbands.

THE DEPARTURE

The bride then retires, in company with her mother and the chief bridesmaid, to change from her wedding finery into her going-away clothes.

As she mounts the stairs to the bedroom set aside for this purpose, it is traditional for the bridesmaids to gather at the foot or below the banisters – while the rest of the wedding party stands by to watch the fun.

From a convenient place on the stairs, the bride throws her bouquet to the young ladies gathered below – and the bridesmaid who captures the bouquet can, reputedly, expect to be the next bride.

While she changes, her baggage is put with the bridegroom's at the exit, all ready to load into the car or taxi that is to take the pair of them on the first stage of the honeymoon.

The bridegroom, if he lives near the venue of the reception (or if one of his friends lives nearby) hurries off with his best man to change into his own going-away clothes. If this is not possible, the bridegroom usually finds a convenient spot among the reception rooms – and as his own dressing should take very much less time than that of his wife, he should be all ready and waiting when she comes down the stairs.

While he is waiting, the bridegroom collects from his best man the rail, steamer or air tickets and any other travel documents that he needs for the honeymoon.

When the bride is ready no further time should be wasted in which emotional scenes may arise. In the years long gone by partings of this nature were a much more final farewell than they are today. A brides' departure with her husband might mean a separation for years between her and her parents – sometimes, if they were going abroad, perhaps for ever. Tears and sorrow were natural under such circumstances – but modern travel has put the most distant parts of the world within a few short hours of home, and with our present standards of living, it is not likely to be impossible for a young couple to save enough for a visit to their parents once in a while.

The occasion should therefore be joyful and a mother's inevitable tears kept from sight.

The farewells should be brisk, cheery and smiling.

Only after the newlyweds have finally departed for their honeymoon should the guests begin to leave – saying their final good-byes to the host and hostess; the bride's mother and father – until only they and the best man remain behind to clear up the paraphernalia of presents, clothes, wedding cake – and the odds and ends that will surely be forgotten by their owners.

CHAPTER FOURTEEN

AFTER THE SHOW . . .

BEFORE leaving the reception rooms the bride's mother should remember to pick up what is left of the wedding cake. Almost certainly the caterer will have packed it in a box strong enough to protect what is left of the sugary confection.

She must gather up, pack and take away with her the wedding clothes left behind by her daughter – and make certain that none of her lady guests has left anything behind.

At the same time the best man will pack and take away the discarded wedding clothes of the bridegroom – and see to it that nothing has been left behind by any of the male guests. He will pocket the telegrams, if he has not already given them to the bride, too.

The best man returns later that afternoon or evening – after he has changed into an every day suit – together with the newlyweds brothers and male friends; armed with boxes, packing cases, paper and string to gather up the collection of wedding presents from the room where they have been exhibited. They are then taken to the home of the bride's parents where they should be put on show in some little used room until such time as they are to be taken to the newlyweds' own home.

On the following day the best man will probably need to return the bridegroom's and his own morning coats and grey trousers to the tailor from whom they have been hired. To purchase outright such clothing is foolish unless it is likely to be used regularly and nowadays it is usually hired.

The bride's mother will settle down to the task of dividing up sufficient of the wedding cake to be able to send a piece to the friends and relatives of the bride and bridegroom who were unable to attend the wedding and the reception afterwards – perhaps because of age, infirmity, illness or distance.

The stationers, from whom the wedding invitation cards were obtained, will provide the tiny boxes in which to pack the segments of cake. A card, fitting the boxes, should have been printed ready to accompany each piece of cake. The wording will probably be as follows, remembering that the address of the sender will be that of the young couple's new home:

Ann Herself

Mr. & Mrs. Peter J. Himself
The Bungalow,
Esher Meade.

With compliments of the occasion of their wedding.

20th April 1969.

It will be seen that the bride's maiden name has been crossed through by a silver arrow – and indeed, all the printing on the card should be in embossed silver.

No acknowledgement of the receipt of the cake should be expected.

On the same day the bride's mother or father should send an announcement of the wedding to the press, for publication in the "Marriages" section of the classified advertisement columns.

It could well read:

HIMSELF : HERSELF – on April 20th at St. George's Parish Church, Woodhouse, Peter John Himself to Ann, daughter of Col. and Mrs. Leslie Herself of Woodhouse, Northumberland.

The local paper is the ideal medium if both the bride and the bridegroom come from the same district; the local paper should be used in each district when the couple come from different parts of the country – and if it should happen that one or other of them was widely known or famous, then publication should be made in one of the national daily newspapers.

The bride's parents must remember that they are expected to make the announcement – not those of the bridegroom. This should be remembered in the case where the bridegroom lived in a different town to that of his bride. It is still her mother's duty to send the announcement to the paper in that town – though it is quite usual for the bridegroom's mother to undertake the task, by mutual agreement.

And the bride's father must settle down to the less pleasant task of paying the bills that will flow in to him. He is generally deemed responsible for the cost of the reception, including everything to do with it; the cake, the bridal gown and the bridesmaids' attire, the meal, the wines, the cars, the flowers – while the bridegroom, or his father, needs to square the much smaller account, usually met on loan by the best man, for the wedding ceremony.

A day or so before the newlyweds are due back from their honeymoon, the bride's parents should take all the wedding presents to their daughter's new home.

As soon as possible after they move in, the bride is expected to start on the task of writing to thank all those who gave her and her husband wedding presents, and to acknowledge the telegrams.

Letters of thanks need to be hand-written; they should neither be printed nor typewritten – however burdensome the duty.

Finally, the last act of the wedding ceremony and ritual takes place spread over the next three months. It is the newlywed's duty to entertain their relatives and friends in their new home. A few at a time, of course, unless the new home is a very large one. Both sets of parents first – after which priority should go to the best man, the bridesmaids and the ushers, though with them, if there is room in the house, other guests may be added.

Then comes the general run of relatives and friends and their entertainment should be settled as a matter of convenience and preference by the bride and bridegroom. The problem is a matter of the numbers to be invited on each occasion and whether the invitation is to tea, to a cocktail party or to dinner.

No mandatory method applies. The couple are at liberty to please themselves – so long as the entertainment is to be in their new house and not outside. On the face of it maiden aunts will prefer to foregather for tea, the friends and relatives of the same generation as the newlyweds, to a cocktail party and the parents and grandparents perhaps to a dinner.

No formal invitation need be sent out. Verbal arrangements or a brief note is sufficient – and acceptances will be returned in the same manner.

CHAPTER FIFTEEN

CHOICE OF MENU FOR THE RECEPTION — AT HOME OR AWAY

LIKES and dislikes are so common where food and drink is concerned that it is only possible to make a few tentative suggestions within the scope of a book of this nature.

Obviously a glance at the tome-like Mrs. Beeton will warn you that the scope is unlimited.

Another point of primary importance before attention is given to the subject of a menu, is where the meal is to be cooked and served.

Certainly, however expert the housewife, it is improbable that her cooking facilities match that of a first class restaurant or hotel. And even if the bride's mother has in mind a menu that can easily be dealt with in her own kitchen, how often is she prepared to undertake the drudgery of cooking and serving such a meal and in consequence having little part in the entertainment itself – even though she is the hostess and should normally never have to leave her guests.

However, it is possible, seasonally, to serve a cold meal which can be prepared in advance, plated and ready to serve from a service table or a sideboard.

For instance, a simple example of this might be:

FRUIT JUICE COCKTAIL

*

COLD ROAST LEG OF LAMB

MINT SAUCE

RUSSIAN SALAD

POTATO SALAD

BEETROOT

*

FRUIT SALAD AND ICE CREAM

*

CHEESE AND BISCUITS

COFFEE

If one preferred a soup served hot, there would be little difficulty in offering, say, Tomato Soup as an alternative to the Fruit Juice Cocktail.

Obviously the alternatives are legion and without much extra work a housewife could permutate an excellent menu from the following short list of suggestions:

CREAM OF CHICKEN NOODLE SOUP

CREAM OF ASPARAGUS SOUP

HONEYDEW MELON

PRAWN COCKTAIL

*

COLD ROAST CHICKEN

COLD ROAST LEG OF PORK

COLD ROAST TURKEY

COLD HAM AND TONGUE

with: RUSSIAN SALAD

POTATO SALAD

BEETROOT

*

FRUIT SALAD AND ICE CREAM
PEACH MELBA
STRAWBERRY MOUSSE WITH CREAM
SHERRY TRIFLE AND ICE CREAM

*

CHEESE AND BISCUITS
TEA OR COFFEE
DESSERT

If the reception is to be held in a hotel or a restaurant, the hostess can be much more ambitious – so long as she is prepared to pay the price for the meal she envisages.

Here are five suggestions for meals that will not cost a great deal; a fish course could be added as an extra:

No. 1.   CREAM OF TOMATO SOUP

*

ROAST CHICKEN WITH BREAD SAUCE
CHATEAU OR CREAMED POTATOES
BRUSSELS SPROUTS
CARROTS VICHY

*

PEACH MELBA

*

COFFEE

No. 2.   CREAM OF ASPARAGUS SOUP

*

ROAST TURKEY WITH FORCEMEAT STUFFING
CHIPPED POTATOES   NEW POTATOES
BUTTERED CABBAGE   GARDEN PEAS

*

STRAWBERRY MOUSSE WITH FRESH CREAM

*

COFFEE

No. 3.   ICED HONEYDEW MELON
          GRILLED HAM STEAK WITH PINEAPPLE
    ROAST POTATOES   CREAMED POTATOES
    WEDGE CARROTS   GARDEN PEAS
                        *

                BANANAS IN JELLY
                        *
                    COFFEE

No. 4.   CREAM OF ASPARAGUS SOUP
                        *

    ROAST AYLESBURY DUCKLING WITH ORANGE SALAD
                        *

    ROAST POTATOES   CREAMED POTATOES
    VICHY CARROTS   PETIT POIS
                        *
                PINEAPPLE CHARLOTTE
                    COFFEE

No. 5.   PRAWN COCKTAIL
                        *

            GRILLED SIRLOIN STEAK GARNI
    CHIPPED POTATOES   CREAMED POTATOES
    BRAISED CELERY HEARTS   MUSHROOMS
    MINTED GARDEN PEAS   FRENCH FRIED ONIONS
                        *
            MIXED FRUIT WITH KIRSCH
                        *
                    COFFEE

Obviously the season has to be taken into consideration, but no doubt the caterer will advise on what is
readily available and in good heart.

It is usual today to offer the guests on their arrival at

the reception a choice of port or sherry certainly and often whisky, gin or almost any other drink immediately available from a dispense bar.

Other hosts make no such provision and have drinks served only with the toasts. Champagne is of course the traditional wedding drink, but there can be no doubt that snob value has had a lot to do with its popularity. The mere fact that it is one of the most expensive wines has given champagne an air of being "right" for such occasions and springs to mind at once.

Other wines are often less favoured because too few people either understand them – or even know them for what they are – yet would often find them more appropriate and certainly less expensive than the commoner champagnes.

Though wine is best consumed in accordance with individual taste, at a function some general rule must be established that is likely to produce the right wine for the majority of the guests. On this principle it is better to offer as an:

aperitif	A dry or medium sherry, a dry Madeira or a light white wine.
with fish	A dry or medium white wine.
with cold meats	A white wine or a light red wine.
with roasts	A white wine with white meat and a red wine with red meat.
with dessert	A sweet table wine such as a Sauterne.

with cheese either Port and perhaps a red Burgundy.

To give a list of wines under each of the headings would require many volumes but a few suggestions may help.

Madeiras are sold today as "dry", "full", "rich" or as the case may be and the name is of less importance than that of the shipper. For an aperitif the Madeira should be "dry" and of the "Sercial" type – and can also be enjoyed with the soup. A sweet Madeira of the "Malmsey" type is ideal with the dessert and is quite suitable as a general wine where no other is to be served during a meal.

A dry or medium sherry, as should be served as an aperitif, may well be a table wine of the "Vino de Pasto" type, though a most popular selection is an "Amontillado".

Among the dry white wines, a choice might be made from amongst the Bordeaux Blanc, such as a Graves; from the White Burgundys, a Chablis; or a Riesling from the Rheingau of Germany.

Sauternes are from Bordeaux and a Barsac from the same region is a popular choice.

Among the red wines a Chateau Claret from the Bordeaux area of France is light and often preferred to a white wine when being served with white meat. A Beaujolais from Burgundy is in the same category, though Burgundy wines are usually considered to have a fuller body and a deeper colour. A Chambertin from the Cote de Nuits vineyards or perhaps a Pommard from the Cote de Beaune will be chosen to be served with red meat or game.

If the reception is to be held in a hotel or a restaurant, the manager will advise what wines are available in his cellar and suggest which of them is most suitable for the chosen meal. Where the reception is to be held in the bride's home or some similar venue, the hostess will be glad to know how many bottles she must buy and a fair guide is:

For a dozen guests two bottles of champagne will be sufficient. (6 to the bottle).

Where wines are drunk a similar number of bottles will be required.

The same number of guests may consume something in the region of one bottle of whisky, one of gin, one of a medium sherry and perhaps a bottle of sweet Martini.

A half dozen of baby tonics, another of ginger ales and two syphons of soda will be needed to mix with the gins and whiskys.

A couple of bottles of cordials should be available too, for children and those of the guests who prefer "soft" drinks.

If at home, supplies on sale or return and the loan of glasses can usually be arranged.

In a hotel or restaurant, the manager will serve the drinks you require and will charge only for the bottles opened – or in the case of spirits, the tots actually served.

Champagnes, white wines and sherrys should be

chilled – two or three hours in cold water will help where no ice or other coolant is available.

Red wines should be served at room temperature by being left on the dining-room sideboard for not less than a couple of hours before they are to be served.

The bottles of wine should be uncorked about an hour before being served to allow the contents to swell.

If more than one wine is to be served, remember that dry white wines should be drunk before both red wines and sweet white wines.

CHAPTER SIXTEEN

SILVER AND GOLDEN WEDDINGS

WEDDING anniversaries are no longer celebrated with the regularity and zest of the years gone by. Generally, the majority of couples remember their first wedding anniversary, sometimes their second and only occasionally their third – after which they tend to become forgotten except perhaps for the exchange of token gifts, such as a bunch of flowers from a husband to his wife.

The wedding anniversaries have always been regarded as a purely private occasion between a man and his wife – except on the rare days when the "silver" or "golden" weddings come around.

Other than those, the anniversaries are usually celebrated with a private party *a deaux*. Perhaps they enjoy themselves for the evening with a dinner followed by a visit to the theatre; maybe a dinner-dance is their choice and sometimes, particularly during the earlier years, they may prefer to distinguish the day with a visit to a night club.

And always, it is an occasion for dressing up, for a taxi and a bottle of wine.

As the years go by the couple tend to gather about

themselves a family and the regular celebrations tend to become a thing of the past. Forgotten perhaps; often made impracticable by the demands of babies.

Even then many couples at least try and mark the day in some small way. An exhange of small presents and perhaps something special for dinner, including an inexpensive wine such as a Sauterne or perhaps a bottle of Barsac.

And still the years slide past and the couple begin to become so absorbed in a welter of such events as children's birthdays, Christmas Days, the school holidays – and in time, their children's own wedding days, that suddenly, almost unbelievably, they find the day approaching when they have completed a quarter of a century of married life. Their Silver Wedding Day.

Something special is called for. First, an announcement in the press, sent by the couple themselves, might read:

> HIMSELF : HERSELF – on 20th April 1940 at St. George's Parish Church, Woodhouse, Peter John Himself to Ann Herself. Present address: The Bungalow, Esher Meade.

Secondly, they will exchange gifts and may expect to receive presents from their family and close friends. Where possible, the presents should consist of silver articles, or where this is not feasible because of cost, particularly gifts from children and grandchildren, the gift should be tied into a parcel with silver ribbon.

The couple may then decide to entertain their children and close friends – and wherever possible, the long ago best man and chief bridesmaid, to a small dinner party.

Formal invitations are not necessary, but they should be issued well in advance so that those who are to be invited may be given time to make their own arrangements.

Formal wear is not usual except in families where it is customary to attend and dress for functions – and the numbers should be restricted to about a dozen.

The venue is usually a hotel or a restaurant and is generally arranged in advance so that a small, private room may be reserved for the occasion.

A wedding cake usually graces the occasion and following the meal, it is cut in the same token fashion as applied on the occasion of the wedding itself, twenty-five years earlier.

Speeches are usually few and happy. The eldest son might propose the "Health and Happiness" of his parents and the husband should reply on behalf of his wife and himself. Other speeches may follow – almost entirely composed of reminiscences – from the best man or one of the guests who was present at the wedding.

The party may go on to a theatre or a dance.

Another quarter of a century may go by and then comes the grand occasion of the Golden Wedding. On this occasion the small party to celebrate the event is usually organized by the eldest son of the couple – often in consultation with his brothers and sisters.

He will make the announcement public through the press, in similar fashion to that published twenty-five years before.

This time the presents should be of gold, though very often they are much less valuable and merely tied up with gold coloured ribbon.

Again the party should be held at a hotel or restaurant if at all possible and equally, if possible, the guests of twenty-five years previously should be invited once again – together with the rising generation of grandchildren.

No formal dress is required nor need any official invitations be sent out. The meal should be ordered with the age of the couple in mind and again a wedding cake is usual though not obligatory.

After the cutting of the cake there may be a few informal speeches – but the husband is not compelled to reply in person. Sometimes the youngest grandson present performs this office for him – though there is no set order of precedence involved.

It is unusual for any sort of entertainment to follow. The guests talk over their cigars and coffee and as soon as the old couple begin to show signs of tiring, the eldest son should bring the proceedings to a close.

It is customary for the eldest son and his wife to escort his parents home. They do not stay when they arrive – and none of the guests should follow.

The Diamond Wedding follows on the anniversary of their sixtieth wedding day – and takes very much the same lines as that described as being applicable to a Golden Wedding. However, the presents almost never consist of diamonds and rarely of anything of more intrinsic value than flowers.

The family party should be kept as small as possible and because of the age of the couple, is usually held either in their own home, or that of one of their children.

The wedding cake need only be a token and as on previous anniversaries, there is no need for pieces of it to be distributed to absent friends and relatives.

The whole celebration must be geared to the ability of the couple to stand up to the fuss – and again, the eldest son and his wife should bring the proceedings to a close as soon as tiredness begins to dull the pleasure of the couple.

As a matter of interest, though of little moment today, anniversaries of a wedding are traditionally known as:

1st anniversary	–	Cotton
2nd	–	Paper
3rd	–	Leather
4th	–	Silk
5th	–	Wood
6th	–	Iron
7th	–	Wool
8th	–	Bronze

9th	–	Pottery
10th	–	Tin
12th	–	Linen
15th	–	Crystal
20th	–	China
25th	–	SILVER
30th	–	Pearl or Ivory
35th	–	Coral
40th	–	Ruby
45th	–	Sapphire
50th	–	GOLD
55th	–	Emerald
60th	–	DIAMOND
75th	–	and again, DIAMOND.

INDEX

INDEX